Front and back cover:
Variety of spices
Slide/Okapia/Reinhard
Pages 2/3:
More spices
Slide/Okapia/Reinhard
Page 7:
Chili peppers and other spices
Page 120 :
Spice mixtures and pastes
Page 128:
Saffron flower
Page 133:
Pepper tree

This edition published in 2002 by
CHARTWELL BOOKS, INC.
A division of Book Sales, Inc
114 Northfield Avenue
Edison, New Jersey 08837

© Molière 2002, Paris
ISBN: 0-7858-1540-6
Printed and bound in Italy
by Grafiche Zanini - Bologna

Photo credits:

Slide/Okapia: 1, 2/3, 7, 11, 23, 24/25, 27, 28/29, 31, 32/33, 34/35, 36/37, 38/39, 41, 43, 44/45, 46/47, 48/49, 51, 53, 55, 56/57, 59, 61, 62, 68/69, 73, 74/75, 76/77, 80/81, 82/83, 118/119, 85, 87, 89, 91, 92/93, 95, 97, 98/99, 101, 103, 104/105, 107, 108/109, 111, 113, 115, 116/117, 129, 136.
Slide: 7.
Slide/Petri: 8.
Slide/APA: 64/65.
Slide/Bernuzeau: 70/71.
Slide/Bianquis: 66/67.
Slide/Ravasini: 78/79.
Slide/Evans: 120.
Tallandier Archives: 15, 16/17.
Private collection, D.R.: 11, 13, 19, 120, 128, 133.

Text: E. Lemoine
Collaboration: F. B. S.B.

SPICES

Elizabeth Lemoine

Foreword
Françoise Izrael

CHARTWELL
BOOKS, INC.

SPICES

Elizabeth Lemoine

Foreword
Françoise Izrael

FOREWORD

Cinnamon, cardamom, coriander, cumin, ginger, nutmeg, allspice, pepper, sandalwood, sesame, sumac... so many spices, among so many species, eliciting familiar and unfamiliar colors, flavors, and aromas. The spice stand at the market draws our attention and delights our senses. In the small shops where they are sold, their fragrances are intensified by the enclosed space, enticing our imagination to wander to exotic places.

The journey of spices was often similar in the past to exploratory expeditions to the four corners of the earth, while the mystery which surrounded their origin was a jealously guarded secret. Today these precious ancestral commodities present a true paradox: on the one hand, they profit from the advantages of globalization by being available everywhere; and on the other hand, traditional trading habits have been preserved: spices are bought and sold in small amounts, sometimes even only less than one ounce at a time - as if they were gold.

Ever since a Chinese emperor recommended the daily use of spices to keep the body's balance five thousand years ago, spices have remained the most traditional and mysterious of goods. As seeds and grains, pastes and powders, separately or mixed, they appear every day in our diet, enriching the flavors of our food.

Their abundance and diversity are so great that it is impossible to compile an exhaustive inventory, and, even if each spice may be used in a thousand different ways, even if traditional recipes detail ingredients and quantities, it is possible, day by day, to vary the amounts and the mixtures to create new recipes and flavors.

Françoise IZRAEL

CONTENTS

FOREWORD: Françoise IZRAEL   *9*

A BRIEF HISTORY OF SPICES   *12*

SPICES AS REMEDIES   *20*

SPICES FROM A TO Z   *22*

SPICE MIXTURES AND PASTES   *121*

INDEX OF SPICES   *130*
Latin and English names

BIBLIOGRAPHY   *132*

A BRIEF HISTORY OF SPICES

Turning an Old Man into a Young Lad:

"Take two hectoliters of fenugreek seeds, grind them and dry them in the sun. Winnow them, in order to separate the grains from the chaff. Measure the amount of seeds, and pass the husks through a sieve in order to keep only the finest part. From these take an amount equal to that of the seeds.

Mix the seeds and the remains of the husks with water to obtain a smooth paste.

Place the paste in a new pot and heat it until the water begins to evaporate: the paste should look like dry mud.

Remove it from the heat and let it cool. When the paste is cold, place it in an earthen pot and rinse it under cold water. It is ready when the water doesn't have any trace of bitterness. Remove the paste from the earthen pot and leave it to dry in the sun on meticulously white washed cloths. Once it is dry, crush it in a mortar, add water and mix it into a smooth paste.

Heat in a caldron until little sheets of oil begin to appear. Remove this oil with a spoon. Take a clay pot, of one deciliter capacity, and make it airtight by covering it with muslin. Pour the oil through it. Gather the purified, filtered mixture in a carefully chosen bowl. Anoint the patient with it.

A massage with this recipe stimulates and refreshes. Baldness, redness, wrinkles, and aging spots will all disappear. This recipe has already been applied successfully millions of times."

This Egyptian recipe is believed to have originated in the New Kingdom (16th to 9th century BC) and is therefore at least 35 centuries old. It is in some respects interesting that not a single scribe has ever documented its actual results. How many old people (and in those times, at what age was a person considered to be old?) regained their youth through its application, is unknown.

This praise to **fenugreek** makes it clear that trying to delay the aging process has always been a concern of mankind. It also shows that, even in very early times, people knew the value of using different spices. Even when this recipe falls between the mysteries of alchemy and plain common sense, it shows how difficult it is, even today, to separate the use of spices as a condiment from their many other uses.

Spices stimulate the organism, enhance the flavor of meals, purify the air, have an influence on people's emotional state and are even present in religious ceremonies. Since their discovery, these tiny, colorful, fragrant grains and leaves have served various purposes. Even 3,000 years before Christ, a Chinese emperor considered them as an indispensable element of his nutrition. Today, in Chinese cuisine, considered to be one of the most refined, there is an impressive number of spicy ingredients being used.

The term spice comes from the Latin *species*, meaning sort or kind. The evolution of the word goes as far back as the Middle Ages, when the term *espice* was used to scientifically identify the different spices used in medical preparations.

Typically, vegetable substances with an aromatic scent and a spicy taste, originating from the root, bark, the fruit, or the dried seeds of a plant, are considered to be spices. These organic parts are often turned into powders or pastes. Some plants are viewed both as herbs and spices. That is true for **aniseed** and **coriander**, of which one can find the leaves or the powdered seeds ready to accomodate dishes. Due to their versatile uses, all the various fragrances from **pepper** to **clove**, from **turmeric** to **cocoa**, from **ginger** to **vanilla**, have been craved for ages.

We know that the Egyptians of the Middle Kingdom (2060–1782 BC) were already familiar with **fenugreek** due to some seeds that were discovered in ceramic objects dating from that time.

The Chinese and the Indians have used spices for more than five thousand years. The well known saying "a healthy spirit lives in a healthy body" is still – somewhat modified – associated with the use of spices as it

Cinnamon
This is one of the oldest spices. Today its fragrantly sweet aroma is used in mulled wine and apple pies.

CANELLA
Canelle

was in those days in the Far East. It has always been about removing the pollutants from the body and the environment to stimulate the organism.

The Egyptians of the Old Kingdom (2572–2130 BC) took great pains to ensure the immortality of their rulers: using colossal stone blocks stones to build the Great Pyramid (the Khufu Pyramid) and other monumental tombs. At the same time, they were concerned with the detailed and careful combination of incense, scents and balms which were used in preserving their mummies. **Pepper** was the only spice that could be identified without doubt.

During the following millennium, the Pharaohs undertook significant expeditions to the East and the South. They developed trading contacts with neighboring nations, such as those on the banks of Euphrates and the Tigris, the Phoenicians, the Cretes, the Mycenaeans and the Greeks. Spices, ointments, oils, and scents formed a considerable part of the goods in which the nations of the Mediterranean traded. The development of Greek pottery supported considerably the shipment of goods, most of all in the area of the Cyclades.

Spices and scents were highly preferred due to the fact that they did not rot. On the island of Crete, living in the palace of **Minos**, there was a certain **Pasiphae** who knew about the preparation of balms. Furthermore, excavations in Mycenae give proof of the importance of fragrances and aromas: **Helen of Troy** and her sister **Clytemnestra** used **coriander**, **aniseed**, **fennel**, **cumin** and **juniper** in dishes, wines or cosmetics.

Spices and scents are also mentioned in the Bible. In Exodus, during the crossing of the desert, when manna fell from heaven: "One could have thought it were **coriander** seeds."

Fragrant goods also played an important role in politics, where they were a part of the gifts exchanged among heads of state. When the Yemenite **Queen of Saba**, well known for her beauty and wisdom, visited her famous neighbor **King Solomon** (King of Israel from 972 to 932 BC), the caravan transported apart from numerous other gifts "a multitude of spices of a magnitude he had never seen before."

Around the same time in the 9th century, aromatic plants and spices became popular through the *Atharvaveda*, where their use was recommended for nutritional purposes in order to stabilize the natural balance of the body.

During the 7th century the trade with incense and spices in the area between the Mediterranean and wealthy Arab countries was dominated by a group of nomads, who eventually settled there. This profitable trade made it possible for them to conquer the city of Petra, the capital of the Edomites. Through the centuries their power grew so much, that even the Romans had to negotiate with them. **Caligula** left them the city of Damascus, but in 106 AD **Trajan** subjugated them and annexed this province to Arabia.

Because of the conquests of **Alexander the Great**, a trade route to the Far East, which had been unreachable before, was established. Later on, Alexandria became the center of the east-west trade under the Ptolemaic rulers of Egypt. Additionally Palmyra played an important role as a meeting point for the caravans of the desert and western traders.

At the time of **Caesar Augustus**, the Arabs dominated the spice trade. They controlled the important trade routes and travelled to the Far East to purchase goods. Once the Romans discovered the appeal and value of spices, they devoted every effort to gain control of the market. However, "*Caius Caesar, son of Augustus, has seen Arabia only from a distance.*"

Evidently, Roman logistics had to surrender to the eastern traders who used to negociate with caravan leaders. **Pliny the Elder** reported that in Arabia "*the richest had been the citizens of the Kingdom of Saba, due to their forest full of aromatic trees, their gold mines, their irrigation system and their culture.*" Furthermore, they guarded their secrets. A little later Pliny explained that, "*incense is only to be found in Arabian countries, but not even in all of them ... At first the people of the Minaean Kingdom traded with incense and they are still the most active traders. Therefore, incense is also known as minaeic. Those are the only Arabs who know the incense tree which does not thrive everywhere. It is said that its culture is an inherited privilege of 3,000 families whose members are called consecrated.*"

Later he pleases us with his observations on **myrtle**: "*I don't know if myrtle was the first tree to be planted on public places, but this would be a remarkable prophetic act.*"

"*The oldest temple is the one of Quirinus, therefore the one of Romulus himself. In front of this temple two myrtle trees, which lived for a long time, were planted. One of them was known as the patrician myrtle, the other as the plebeian myrtle. For a long time the*

Cõment li rois assuares tiut court 7 le roine vasti aulli
Le roine vasti le femme le roi assuare tiut court des dames
du roiaume v palais du roi · aulli q̃ li rois le tenoit des hõmez

patrician myrtle was the stronger one. When the senate was flourishing, the plant was marvelous. On the other hand, the plebeian one was in poor health and dying. However, during war times, the power of the senate was weak and the majestic tree slowly withered."

The famous Roman cook **Apicius** too held spices in high esteem. He particularly liked **pepper** in all colors and preparations: whole and crushed or as fine powder. He also recommended, **saffron**, **ginger**, **clove**, **lemonbalm**, **poppy seed**, **wormwood**, **coriander**, **cumin**, and **aniseed**.

To the Romans, spices symbolized exotic and oriental magic. Most of decadent Rome indulged itself in the aromatic substances, as Petronius testifies. **Nero**, upon entering the city, had the streets of Rome covered with a wasteful abundance of **roses** and **saffron**, corresponding to the annual consumption of its citizens. During their conquests, the Romans brought spices to northern Europe, but with the end of the Empire the trade in spices subsided. The Vandals and Huns had no interest in a high level lifestyle. Nevertheless, the new eastern capital, Constantinople, was adding the magic and aromas of the orient to its wealth. With the conquest of Spain by the Moors and the return of the Crusaders, a breeze of the orient finally arrived in the western world.

Later on, when Genoa and Venice were competing against each other to be the most important port for east-west trade, spices again became lucrative trade goods. In Europe, a time of upheaval and changing fashions followed. Consumption of meat was increasing,

as well as the consumption of **pepper** and **saffron** which, as in Rome, were considered to be medicinal. In addition to the sweet-salty flavors of Medieval times, the flavors of spices received such an impetus that they were present in most dishes. In the 12th century, **Taillevent**, chef of **Charles VI**, wrote in Le Viandier suggestions on how to use spices. In his day, the principal object of using spices was to disguise the flavor of food which, due to the lack of refrigeration, was frequently tainted. Thus, one of his recipes for a thick and jam-like sauce using vinegar and **cinnamon**, might be unedible today. Spices were sold like gold, making the Italian merchants rich. In the 13th century, the rich Venetian merchants **Niccolò** and **Matteo**, uncle and father of **Marco Polo**, were the first to trade with spices from China. At the beginning of the 15th century, **pepper** and **ginger** were the number one imported spices.

The hunt for these exotic powders lasted a few centuries and led to various conflicts. In 1497, the Portuguese **Vasco da Gama** sailed from Lisbon with four caravels to India. He circumnavigated Africa, reaching the coast of Malabar. After the discovery of this route, various other expeditions followed, which made the Portuguese the rulers of the Moluccas, also known as the "Spice Islands." Then they headed on to Ceylon, from where they brought considerable amounts of spices to Europe, and soon had the monopoly of the market.

The wonderful discoveries of **Marco Polo** made the Genoese **Christopher Columbus** dream. We all know the story. He wanted to sail to India in order to find a direct route to the "Spice Islands." Instead, he

Pepper

Be it Apicius in Rome, the lady of the castle in Medieval times, or the modern chef: pepper is used regularly every where. Pepper is also one of the few spices used to pay French judges.

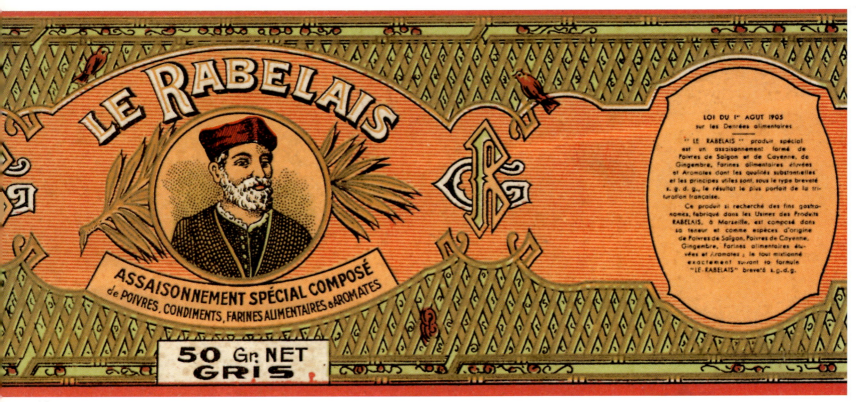

discovered America and returned with **chili-pepper** and **vanilla**. The Dutch and the British were fast to make a profit from it. The Dutch displaced the Portuguese from the market and, in 1602, founded the influential East India Company. **Elizabeth I** laid the foundations of the British Empire. In 1600, the British East India Company acclimatized **nutmeg** and **cloves** in Malaysia and developed the cultivation of spices in Singapore. In 1664 the French settled in India. Minister of finance **Colbert** supported the trade and founded the French *Compagnie des Indes* with headquarters in Pondichéry.

The French priest **Pierre Poivre** (1719–86) undertook long missionary voyages. Later he quit the priesthood and joined the Asia Trade Company. He was responsible for the procurement of **clove**, **cinnamon**, and **nutmeg** plants in order to acclimatize them on the Bourbon islands and the island of Mauritius. From 1767 to 1773 he was the governor of Mauritius. He travelled to the Moluccas, deceived the Dutch and dug out wild-growing plants, whose seeds had been spread by birds. He accomplished the mission and spices could now be cultivated as well on the islands of the Indian Ocean and on Zanzibar, which is still today one of the main producers of **cloves**. **Poivre** travelled around the world and, in 1770, introduced **pepper** as a new spice. He procured the young plants from the Dutch colonies. The similarity of his name with the French word *poivre* for **pepper** is a mere coincidence. Later he built the botanical garden *Jardin des Pamplemousses* on the Ile de France.

In the 18th century, spices were considered an exquisite delicacy offered to judges. In the beginning it was just a gesture of politeness, which in time became a duty. Thus, in France, spices stood for "judge's fee." This practice ended in 1798 with the revolution. At the end of the 18th century, the British consolidated their supremacy by conquering India and Ceylon. The British managed to force their rivals out of the spice trade routes, but spices were not that rare anymore.

Around the same time, the United Sates entered the market importing huge amounts of **pepper** from Sumatra through the ports of Salem (Massachusetts) and New York. The big traders founded their famous companies. **Fortnum & Mason** provided London with spices and other precious products. In 1850 **Hédiard** founded in France a spice and colonial produce store. In 1886 **Fauchon** founded his fine spice business at the Place de la Madeleine in Paris and **Jacob Hooy** founded in the Netherlands an herb and drug business.

In the 19th century spices became less and less a precious commodity. Numerous countries produced them and transportation became easier. New packaging technologies (jars, bags) allowed for better conservation.

Today spices are shipped daily in the main ports of London, Rotterdam, Hamburg, Singapore and New York. Nevertheless, the spice trade is still important worldwide. **Pepper**, **cardamom** and **piment** are at the top of the list. Generally speaking, there are four main spice producing regions: Asia produces **cloves**, **pepper**, **ginger** and others; the Mediterranean region is known for **mustard**, **poppy** seed and **fennel**; America produces **vanilla** and **chili**; and northern Europe produces **juniper** and **caraway**.

SPICES AS REMEDIES

CARDIO-VASCULAR SYSTEM

ANAEMIA - CHINA BARK *wine.*

ARTERIOSCLEROSIS - SOY BEAN *in all its forms.*

BLOOD CLOTS - BLACK MUSTARD *compress.*

BRUISES - PAPAYA *as fruit,* MYRTLE *essential oil.*

CHOLESTEROL - *all foods should be* SOY BEAN *based.*

CIRCULATION - *ginger tea.*

DIABETES - FENUGREEK *in infusions and as a nutritional supplement.*

HAEMORRHOIDS - MYRTLE *juice.*

HEART PROBLEMS - COLA *tonic wine,*
GARLIC *in various dishes,*
CAMPHOR *as a stimulant.*

HIGH BLOOD PRESSURE - GREEN TEA *leaves in infusions, garlic and
soy bean in as many dishes as possible, orange jasmine.*

MEMORY LOSS - SOY BEAN *germ or milk.*

PHLEBITIS - GARLIC *in as many dishes as possible.*

DIGESTIVE SYSTEM

AEROPHAGIA - AJOWAN, CARAWAY, CUMIN *and* CORIANDER *seeds
with meals or in infusions,* LEMON JUICE *with warm water,*
CARDAMOM *seeds as seasoning.*

APPETITE STIMULANTS - FENUGREEK *seeds,* TURMERIC, PEPPER
and CALUMBA, VANILLA.

APPETITE SUPPRESSANTS - CASSIA, BETEL PALM PITH.

COLITIS - FENNEL SEED DECOCTION.

CONSTIPATION - LEMON, GRAPEFRUIT, ORANGE *and* OTAHEITE GOOSEBERRY
eaten raw, MALLOW *infusions,* TAMARIND *pith.*

DIARRHEA - *infusions with* POMEGRANATE *and* CINNAMON, CASSIA *pulp,*
CORNELIAN *cherry juice,* GAMBIER.

DIGESTION - BOLDO *and* BITTER ORANGE *leaf infusions,*
PAPAYA: *use the leaves in infusions and eat the fresh fruit.*

DYSENTERY - ANATTO *leaf infusions, ripe fruit
from the screw pine tree.*

GASTRITIS - CUMIN *and* CORIANDER *seeds in a decoction
or as seasoning,* NUTS *from the* CANDLE NUT TREE.

INDIGESTION - BLACK CUMIN *infusions or used as seasoning.*

NAUSEA, STOMACH PAIN - FENNEL *in infusions or as seasoning,*
PEPPER *as seasoning, candied* GINGER.

SLOW STOMACH - CUMIN, CALUMBA, CORIANDER, LEMON,
FENNEL *as seasoning,* GREEN ANISEED *liqueur,*
CORNELIAN CHERRY BARK *juice,* UNCARIA.

STOMACH CRAMPS - *decoction of* FENNEL *seeds.*

VOMITING - CASSIA *pith.*

RESPIRATORY SYSTEM

BRONCHITIS - *inhalation with* EUCALYPTUS LEAVES,
LICORICE *to chew,*
as a paste, or in a decoction and ground, raw HORSERADISH
or HORSERADISH *syrup.*

COUGH - EUCALYPTUS *to inhale,*
MALLOW *syrup (blossoms and leaves)*
or CANDY, LICORICE *to chew or in a decoction.*

DRY MOUTH - BOLDO *leaves in a decoction.*

EMPHYSEMA, ASTHMA - JUNIPER BERRY, *as* SEASONING,
in a decoction, and to inhale.

INFLUENZA - CHINA BARK TREE *wine.*

LARYNGITIS - MYRTLE, *fresh or in juice.*

URINARY SYSTEM

AMENORRHEA - SAFFRON *and* ASAFETIDA *infusions.*

LEUCORRHEA - DOUCHE *with an infusion of* POMEGRANATE *leaves.*

SEXUAL FATIGUE - *ginger: fresh, candied or in a decoction.*

NERVOUS SYSTEM

ANXIETY - *infusions of* POPPY *seed or as nutritional supplement,*
POPPY *blossom and* GREEN COFFEE BEAN *syrup.*

ASTHMA - HORSERADISH *syrup,* ALMONDS *from the* CANDLE NUT TREE.

INSOMNIA - *infusions of* MALLOW *and* ORANGE *blossoms.*

NERVOUS SPASM - ANISEED *infusions.*

NERVOUSNESS - *infusions with* GREEN ANISEED.

NEURALGIA, SYNCOPE - *compresses with* BLACK MUSTARD.

RHEUMATISM - *warm raw, ground* HORSERADISH *rubbed on the skin.*

MOUTH PROBLEMS

ABSCESSES, CAVITIES - CLOVES *crushed or as an essence,*
ROSE PEPPER *leaves.*

GINGIVITIS - *rinse with diluted* SWEET ORANGE *juice.*

TOOTH ACHE - *crushed* PEPPER *seeds,* GINGER.

MUSCULO-SKELETAL SYSTEM

JOINT PAIN - POPPY *leaves in warm compresses,*
fresh CERIMAN *juice.*

MUSCLE PAIN - RAVENSARA *leaves balm,*
CINNAMON *or* JUNIPER *oil to massage.*

RHEUMATISM - *massage with* CINNAMON *or* JUNIPER *oil,*
decoction with BARK *from the root of* SASSAFRAS.

LIVER DISORDERS

GALL BLADDER - GREATER GALANGA, *fresh or in powder as nutritional
supplement, shell* GINGER *stimulates gall bladder activity.*

HEPATIC INSUFFICIENCY - *infusions with* BOLDO *leaves,*
HORSERADISH *as syrup and seasoning.*

**LIVER STRAINING, DISORDERS OF THE LIVER
AND GALL BLADDER FUNCTION** - TURMERIC *used as decoction
and as a seasoning.*

DISORDERS OF THE SKIN

ACNE - *compresses with an infusion of* SWEET GALE.

IRRITATION - ROSE *water,* HORSERADISH *tree oil,*
compresses with crushed MYRTLE *or* SESAME *leaves.*

DISORDERS OF THE KIDNEYS AND BLADDER

KIDNEY STONES - *decoction with* FENUGREEK *and* BOLDO.

KIDNEY AND BLADDER INSUFFICIENCY - CASSIA *pulp,* JUNIPER *wine,*
CUMIN, FENNEL *and* FENUGREEK *as food supplements
freshly ground* HORSERADISH *as a seasoning.*

EYE DISORDERS

INFLAMMATION - *eyewash with a decoction
of* SESAME *leaves.*

OTHER AILMENTS

BRUISES, SCRAPES AND SCRATCHES - *compresses with crushed* BLACK PEPPER.

EXHAUSTION AND FATIGUE - *fresh or candied* GINGER *root*, CANDLE NUT TREE.

FEVER - CHINA BARK TREE *wine, decoction of blossoms and leaves of the* ORANGE TREE, ANNATTO *and* SUMAC.

HEADACHE - *compresses with fresh* GINGER.

INADEQUATE MILK SUPPLY - *infusions of* FENNEL *seeds.*

MICROBE INFESTATION - *fresh* GARLIC *in the kitchen,* LEMON *juice as a drink or to rub wounded area, compresses with* RAVENSARA *leaves,* GALANGA *and* CARDAMOM.

NICOTINE ADDICTION - *infusions with fresh* COFFEE *leaves,* EUCALYPTUS *leaves to smoke,* BETEL PALM *tablets to chew.*

OVERWEIGHT, CELLULITIS - *fresh* GRAPEFRUIT, *fresh* PAPAYA, BLACK TEA.

PHYSICAL AND EMOTIONAL EXHAUSTION - COLA *seed drink.*

SCURVY - GARLIC, CITRIC FRUITS, *plenty of* HORSERADISH, WINTER'S BARK, *fresh* MANGO.

TRAVEL SICKNESS - *fresh* GINGER *in infusions or candied.*

PARASITES

AMOEBAS - PAPAYA *seeds.*

WORMS - ANATTO *seeds,* PAPAYA *and* CLEOME, *decoction of the blossoms and the bark of* SOUR ORANGE.

GLOSSARY OF MEDICAL PROPERTIES

ANTISCORBUTIC: *fights scurvy.*

ANTISEPTIC : *stops infections and destroys microbes.*

ANTISPASMODIC: *see calmant.*

APPETITIVE : *stimulates the appetite.*

ASTRINGENT : *diminishes the secretions of glands and mucous membranes.*

BALSAMIC : *stimulates the digestive and respiratory tracts.*

BECHIC : *calms coughs, irritations of the respiratory system and facilitates expectoration.*

CALMANT : *acts on the nervous system.*

CARMINATIVE : *favors the elimination of gas and calms stomach pains.*

CHOLAGOGUE : *facilitates release of the bile from the gall bladder.*

DEMULCENT : *allays irritation of surfaces, especially mucous membranes.*

DEPURATIVE : *removes impurities from the blood.*

DIURETIC : *favors elimination of urine.*

EMETIC : *favors vomiting.*

EMMENAGOGUE : *provokes, facilitates menstrual flow.*

EMOLLIENT : *soothes and calms inflammation of tissues.*

FEBRIFUGE : *lowers fevers.*

GALACTOGENIC : *favoring milk production.*

HEMOSTATIC : *stops bleeding.*

PURGATIVE : *cleans the intestines.*

RESOLUTIVE : *relaxes and softens swollen tissues.*

STIMULANT : *augments energy of the vital functions.*

STOMACHIC : *excites the appetite.*

SUDORIFIC : *favors perspiration.*

TONIC : *strengthens the organism.*

VULNERARY : *externally, heals wounds; internally, combats physical weakness.*

GLOSSARY OF TECHNICAL TERMS

ACHENE : *dry fruit that does not open by itself.*

ALTERNATE : *leaves arranged at different levels on the stem; one leaf to a node.*

ANNUAL : *a plant whose life cycle from germination to maturity and death lasts only one growing season.*

AXIL : *the angle between the stem and the leaf stalk.*

BERRY : *fleshy fruit with pips.*

BIENNIAL : *a plant whose life cycle lasts two growing seasons.*

BIPINNATE : *leaves formed of pinnate divisions, themselves formed of pinnate leaflets.*

BRACT : *leaf at the base of a flower, usually much reduced in size.*

CARPEL : *female organ of the flower.*

CATAPLASM : *poultice.*

COLIC : *severe stomach pain.*

COMPRESS : *wet cloth put on a wound to relieve inflammation.*

CORYMB : *an almost flat-topped inflorescence.*

CRENATE : *scalloped; with blunt teeth.*

CROWN : *the flowering extremity of a plant.*

CUPULE : *a series of closed bracts that form a cup beneath the fruit.*

CYME : *a flower cluster in the shape of an inverted cone.*

DECOCTION : *a preparation made by putting the plant in cold water and heating to a boil.*

DEHISCENT : *said of a fruit that opens at maturity.*

DENTATE : *toothed (leaf margin).*

DIACHENE : *a double achene carried on a single peduncle.*

DIOECIOUS : *having male and female flowers on separate plants.*

ENTIRE : *not in any way indented; featureless margin.*

EVEN-PINNATE : *compound leaf with an even number of leaflets.*

GLAUCOUS : *bluish-green.*

HEAD : *a dense, spherical or rounded inflorescence of sessile flowers, as in the composite family.*

INFLORESCENCE: *axes along which all the buds are flower buds.*

INFUSION : *an herbal tea prepared by pouring boiling water on the plant and allowing to stand for 5 to 10 minutes.*

LEAFLET : *division of a compound leaf.*

MONOECIOUS : *a plant bearing both male and female flowers.*

ODD-PINNATE : *leaf having an uneven number of leaflets with a terminal leaflet.*

PANICLE : *flower-cluster in which the terminal flowers open last.*

PEDICEL : *the stem of one flower in a cluster.*

PEDUNCLE : *small ramification of the stem ending in a flower.*

PERENNIAL : *said of a plant that survives several years and that flowers every year, the aerial parts disappearing each winter.*

PETIOLATE : *having a petiole or leaf stalk.*

PINNATE : *feather-like; leaflets arranged along a central leaf axis.*

RHIZOME : *perennial subterranean stem.*

ROSETTE : *a radiating leaf cluster at or near the base of the plant.*

RUNNER : *an aerial, trailing shoot, the tip of which takes root when it touches the ground.*

SAMARA : *a winged achene.*

SESSILE : *attached directly to the stem without a peduncle.*

SHEATHING : *enclosure of the stem by a sheath-like leaf.*

SILIQUE : *dehiscent fruit opening in four parts.*

SIMPLE : *a cultivated aromatic or medicinal plant.*

SIMPLE LEAF : *a leaf that is not divided into leaflets.*

SOLITARY : *with a single flower.*

SPADIX : *inflorescence surrounded by a large bract.*

SPIKE : *an inflorescence with a single axis and flowers without pedicels.*

STOLON : *creeping aerial or subterranean stem by which the plant propagates.*

TETRACHENE : *quadruple achene.*

UMBEL : *an umbrella-shaped inflorescence of few to many flowers on pedicels of approximately equal length.*

THESE NATURAL REMEDIES ARE NOT BY ANY MEANS INTENDED TO REPLACE MEDICINES PRESCRIBED BY A DOCTOR.

SPICES FROM A TO Z

<table>
<tr><td>ACACIA CATECHU</td><td align="right">Cutch or Betel palm</td></tr>
</table>

Family: *Mimosaceae*
Origin: *Bengal, Sri Lanka and East Africa*
Height: *32.8 feet (10 m)*
Flowering: *at the end of the tropical winter*
Properties: *antidiarrhoea, antihaemorragic, astringent, invigorating, tonic*

Betel palm has been used in India for tanning purposes. It yields a shiny, reddish-brown, resinous extract known as **cutch**. This extract which has medicinal properties is obtained from the trunk of fallen trees. The wood is chopped into pieces that are later cooked in water. The decoction is then filtered and set aside until the water has evaporated leaving a resinous substance – **cutch** – behind.

From afar, the tree resembles a Mimosa. It has distinctive bipinnate leaves, with small, pale, yellow flowers which are arranged in compact globular clusters. **Cutch** has a pleasant, bittersweet taste. It is rich in tannin and vitamins. Among the several varieties of **cutch**, there is **yellow cutch**, from Batavia and **brown cutch** from Calcutta. However, the most sought out variety is found in Pegu (Burma).

Cutch is available in two different forms: in bread or in tiny capsules, which are often scented with cinnamon, rose, mint, or orange leaves.

Cutch tablets are reputed to refresh breath and are especially recommended for smokers. They are also used to calm pangs of hunger or when trying to quit smoking.

Cutch can be easily dissolved in hot water, alcohol and vinegar, and can be used as a dye. Cotton and wool colored with **cutch** take on a soft brown color.

Cutch

The tiny cutch capsules are used in fruit salads, plum compote, and to garnish baked goods.

<table>
<tr><td>AGATHOPHYLLUM</td><td align="right">Ravensara, Madagascar or Clove nutmeg</td></tr>
</table>

Family: *Lauraceae*
Origin: *Madagascar*
Height: *32 to 49 feet (10 to 15 m)*
Flowering: *early summer*
Properties: *antiseptic, sedative, stimulant, sudorific*

This tree, which belongs to the same family as the **camphor** and bay trees, also has an intense aroma. It is an evergreen tree with cylindrical branches which carry leaves on short stems. Its hermaphrodite flowers are very small and have a unilocular ovary containing only one ovule. Once it has bloomed, **ravensara** produces fragrant berries with a dark blue shell.

Ravensara is aromatic and stimulating. The leaves are used as a spice. The berries are harvested fresh and have a pleasant scent and a tangy spicy flavor. The leaves and fruit of this tree are very popular spices.

The leaves of **ravensara** contain essential oils, tannin, bitter essence, and lipids. Used in a decoction, they ease digestion and help fight tiredness. They are also used in a compress to disinfect wounds and applied as an ointment to soothe muscle pain.

In the kitchen, its leaves are used to season ragouts, stocks, soups, meat, fish and vegetable dishes, while the fresh fruit may be added to heighten their taste and aroma. When it is dry, it is crushed and used like **pepper**. More practically, its very fragrant leaves can be spread around the house in order to keep annoying insects away.

ALEURITES MOLUCCANA — Candle nut tree, Tung tree

Family: Euphorbiaceae
Origin: South China, Indonesia, Hawaii
Height: 49 feet (15 m)
Flowering: early summer
Properties: relieves asthma, anti-fatigue, tranquilizer, carminative, sedative

This tree of frail foliage is also known as **tung tree**. The **candle nut** is a medium-sized tree with a soft fuzzy bark that looks as if it had been sprinkled with flour. It has long, three lobed leaves.

Its white flowers are disposed on terminal clusters. Even though male and female flowers are usually borne on the same plant, they are easily identified. Its fruit is used in the making of a spice known as inanome.

Its great rounded or oval seeds sit on a long stem and are made, like walnuts, of a wooden like shell with an inner, cotton wool, fibrous coating and an oily, split grain. Flowers, nuts and bark owe their medicinal properties to their internal components. They are reputed to be good for general weakness and exhaustion. Furthermore, they alleviate pain and ulcers, and relieve asthma attacks. Due to their effect on the nervous system, they are also used to reduce abdominal bloating and constipation. The nuts contain oil that is used in Asia as lubricating oil, lamp oil, and in the manufacturing of candles and soaps. In addition, it is used in the production of fast drying and weather resistant varnishes for floors and boats. From the shell and the juice of the fruit, a tincturelike substance is extracted.

Candle nut trees are to some extent grown for commercial purposes. The roasted nuts are crushed and mixed with **salt** to produce a seasoning known as inanome. It is used to give aroma to fish ragouts, meat and vegetable dishes. Because the **candle nut tree** plays such an important economic role in Hawaii, it was chosen as the "national tree" in 1959.

ALPINIA GALANGA — Greater galanga

Family: Zingiberaceae
Origin: Indonesia
Height: blossom stems can reach up to 6.5 feet (2 m)
Flowering: summer
Properties: antibacterial, expectorant, laxative, stimulant

Greater galanga

This spice with its delicate aroma is greatly treasured in the south eastern parts of Asia. It is used in curry mixtures to season meat and poultry. It is combined with other ingredients such as onions, garlic, chili peppers and ginger into a paste used in soups and ragouts. In Europe and Scandinavia, it is used in the production of beer and some liqueurs. In former times, it was also used as a scent for vinegar. This tropical plant is quite big and beautiful. The variety Alpina Vitatta, from the Pacific Islands, is especially decorative.

Among the **galanga** official species there are two varieties: the **greater** and **lesser galanga**. Even though both species are related to **ginger**, **lesser galanga** is less known and is only grown in those countries from where it originates.

The fleshy, aromatic, roots have a light creamy color, the majority with brown ringlike veining. Its perennial leaves have a distinct lancelike form which,

from afar, could be taken for those of a banana or canna tree.

Its flowers are white, often reddish, very thin and relatively big. They appear on long, strong branches and hang casually over them. Small capsulelike fruit in various lines of red grow out of them.

The rhizomes of the **galanga** are considered to be one of the most important spices in Java and Malaysia. Harvesting is done by digging out the roots which are immediately dried in the sun. The **galanga** has a delicate fragrance, similar to that of the pine, and quite a spicy taste. All together it resembles a mixture of juniper and **pepper**.

Fresh and dry, powdered **galanga** is to be found in gourmet stores. The fresh rhizomes can be kept in the refrigerator up to two weeks when packed in a paper bag.

The powder should be stored in an airproof container away from light in order to preserve its aroma.

Greater galanga, which contains essential oils and tannin, is used as an antibacterial agent. Because it regulates the gall bladder function, it also helps the digestive system. In addition, it is used to relieve respiratory illnesses.

In India, galanga is eaten to counter bad breath. It can also be used as a remedy for nervous exhaustion and is well known for its aphrodisiac properties.

ALPINIA OFFICINARUM **Lesser galanga**
Family: Zingiberaceae
Origin: Southern China (Hainan Island)
Height: 3.2 to 5 feet (1 to 1,5 m) high and 3.2 feet (1 m) wide
Flowering: summer
Properties: digestive, tonic

Although the **lesser galanga** is a close relative of the **greater galanga**, it differs from it in its size. It too has fleshy rhizomes with a very fibrous structure. It contains volatile oils and tannin which give it a spicy fragrance, distantly reminiscent of that of **eucalyptus**.

Its taste borders between spicy and hot, comparable to that of **pepper**. It is especially treasured in Asian dishes, where it is used in moderation. The rhizomes are also used in the production of curries and liqueurs.

Far less known is the *Kaempferia galanga* variety, which is employed by specialized spice dealers only. The differences that set it apart from the other two are minor. Instead of roots, it has an ocher brown rootstock with fleshy tubers (storage organs) and its many branched stem bears long narrow sheaths. Its properties and uses are similar to those of the other well known **galanga** species.

ANETHUM GRAVEOLENS **Dill**
Family: Umbelliferae
Origin: Asia Minor
Height: 15.7 to 27.5 inches (40 to 70 cm)
Flowering: spring
Properties: apéritif, aromatic, sedative, carminative

This annual aromatic plant is very popular in the Mediterranean region and can be found regularly in kitchen gardens throughout Europe. Occasionally it is preferred to **fennel** (*Foeniculum vulgare*), to which it is closely related. Today, **dill** is mainly grown in North America (USA and Mexico) and Asia (India and China).

Dill has been known since antiquity. Like mint, **fennel** and **cumin**, **dill** was treasured by the ancient Hebrews who imposed a tax on it. The Roman gladiators, before going to battle, rubbed their bodies with an oil that contained a **dill** extract.

The plant has upright, ribbed, hollow, branches. The bluish leaves are compound and featherlike. The yellow blossoms spring from the stalks like the ribs of an umbrella. Brown seeds that in the summer become ripe, develop inside. **Dill** grows wild on the side of the road and in fallow land. In the garden, this plant requires rich soil with good drainage, and a sunny and dry location. It is grown from seed in the spring and at the beginning of the summer to prolong the harvest. Its leaves, which are cut fresh as needed, and its flowers are used fresh or dried. The seeds are harvested in August and left in a shady, airy place to dry. Afterwards, they can be used whole or crushed.

From the seeds of **dill**, essential oils can be obtained. The plant also contains tannin, resin, slime, magnesium, calcium, iron and vitamin C. The leaves improve digestion and, when used in an infusion, relieve belching and hiccups. The essential oil is known for its soothing effect. **Dill** can be chewed to prevent bad breath. It is also a good replacement for **salt** when a low **salt** diet is required. Like asparagus leaves, **dill** leaves can also be used to fill up flower arrangements.

ARENGA PINNATA **Arenga or Sugar palm**
Family: Arecoidae
Origin: Australia and Southeastern Asia
Height: 65 feet (20 m)
Flowering: summer
Properties: purifier, nutritious, tonic, stimulant

Comprising 17 different species, the **arenga** has an important economic value. The majority of the species are grown in Indonesia on the islands of Sumatra and Java, where, for many years, native people have gathered the juice of the palm and used its parts for domestic purposes.

The **sugar palm** has a massive trunk with ring-like stigma that is covered with a dark, dense fiber which

---

Dill

Due to its sweet spicy taste, dill is quite often used as a seasoning. The seeds are not only used to flavor marinades, sauerkraut, pickles and other vegetables, but also in pastries and bread. The leaves go well with cream cheese, cottage cheese, eggs, seafood, fish (for example, smoked salmon), mutton, and sauces. Dill should always be used fresh because when it is cooked or dried, it loses its aroma. The flowers are added to stews, pickles and carrots.

Horseradish

Horseradish can be used in many different ways. When fresh, its aroma is quite distinct. The dry root has the same properties as the fresh one. Peeled, ground and mixed with crème fraîche it becomes an exquisite relish served along with cold meat, raw or cooked fish, hard boiled eggs, and soups. Freshly ground horseradish is also suitable to flavor and enhance stuffings, purées, sauces, pâtés, carrots and beetroot. When prepared with wine and butter it renders a delicious sauce that goes well with roast beef, poultry, and smoked fish such as Herring and Mackerel. A wonderful paste is obtained by mixing horseradish with ground apples. It can then be served as a relish for game. Young flowers of the horseradish can be used in soups and pickles made of such vegetables as cucumbers and beetroot.

Wasabi

In Japan, there is a variety of horseradish: wasabi (wasabi japonica). It has the same properties as horseradish except that the color of the flesh of the root is more delicate, reminiscent of that of a raw potato. Its roots are used pretty much the same as those of horseradish. A seasoning sauce, used to accompany sushi, fish and several vegetables, is obtained by mixing wasabi powder with water or soy sauce. It is advisable to serve both varieties of horseradish with fatty foods since they facilitate digestion.

is hard and pungent. The trunk of the tree is surmounted by a crown of 24 long and strong featherlike leaves.

Each leaf, which can reach up to 39 feet in length, has a rigid central rib endowed with 150 to 200 long, pointed leaflets. Its flowers, clustered like hanging grapes which can reach up to 6.5 feet in length, are bisexual and bloom from top to bottom. Before blooming, the flowers are enclosed by a number of spathes. They render berrylike fruit containing up to three seeds, the pulp of which is inedible because it contains poisonous oxalate.

The juice and pith are harvested as edible products and the strong fibers are used for domestic purposes. To extract the juice, the young male flowers are carved one by one. Once a flower is emptied, the one below it is split open. The liquid is slowly obtained through a series of successive gashes. Over a period of five months, two to seven liters of juice can be collected per day.

One single palm tree can produce up to 18 liters of sweet juice. This juice is composed of 15% of sucrose, mineral salts, vitamin A and B, and trace elements. It is, therefore, a very nutritious substance.

After fermentation, the juice is used to produce a nourishing wine that when consumed in great amounts may become toxic to the organism. An unrefined **sugar**, which is sold commercially in pressed blocks, is produced by boiling the juice. It is used in the preparation of baked goods, candies, and syrups and to sweeten and flavor drinks.

Sago, a kind of starch that comes in small grains which are easily diluted in milk or water, is obtained from the pith of the **arenga**. It is used to prepare nourishing, light puddings and porridges. It is also mixed in with fish broth, **lemon** juice, and spices to prepare other hearty dishes. Brooms, brushes, mats and wicker objects are manufactured using the solid fibers of the palm.

ARMORACIA RUSTICANA	**Horseradish**

Family: *Cruciferae*
Origin: *Russia and Western Asia*
Height: *4.9 feet (1.5 m)*
Flowering: *May to July*
Properties: *apéritif, bactericide, digestive, purgative, stimulant, tonic*

Horseradish, a hardy perennial plant, was already known to the Slavs and Teutons. Its cultivation goes back as far as the 12th century. Traditional recipes to prepare sauces using this seasoning have been traced back to this period.

In the Middle Ages, the Germans employed it as a **mustard**. Its cultivation spread throughout France during the 16th century, especially in the Alsace region.

In its wild state, **horseradish** grows in humid ground, ditches, and on the banks of streams. This very undemanding plant develops under any given circumstance: it can endure frost and drought, but grows badly in heavy, moist soil.

Its root can reach up to 20 inches in length. It is thick and fleshy with a rugged outer yellow or grey shell and fibrous, white to yellowish pulp. Its stem is erect and widely branched. Its large, coarse, glossy-green basal leaves arise on long stems from the crown atop the large white root. Its very fragrant, small, white flowers are borne in terminal racemes.

Flowering gives rise to the development of a globular fruit which contains flat seeds. The propagation of **horseradish** is mostly done in a vegetative way through its roots. In the spring time, after the third season, the plant is ploughed from the soil and the tufts are trimmed. The pieces of root that are obtained are replanted preferably in lose, sandy soil.

The aromatic **horseradish** root is the plant's most widely used part. It has a hot, burning taste which is more intense than that of **mustard**. In the autumn or in the spring the roots of the plant are harvested. With the help of a pitchfork, the roots are slightly lifted without pulling them out completely.

The roots are then cut off and the plant is buried in the earth again. All but two roots are removed to ensure that the plant regenerates. To preserve the harvested roots, they are placed in a box with sand and stored in a cool, dark place (preferably in the cellar).

This plant is rich in vitamins A and C. It contains essential oils, mineral salts, glucose, sugar, carotene and bactericidal substances. It is a very useful spice during the winter and spring months. Because it contains vitamin C, it helps fight against colds and fatigue. However, it is not recommended for people suffering from nervous disorders, people who have an irritated stomach, or pregnant women.

ASARUM EUROPAEUM   *Wild ginger or Asarabacca*

Family: Aristolochiaceae
Origin: Middle East
Height: 6 to 9.8 inches (15 to 25 cm)
Flowering: end of winter
Properties: aromatic, diuretic, purgative, emetic

Wild ginger is a small dicotyledone plant. It has established itself in the regions of central Europe where it is mainly used as a **ginger** substitute. This delicate plant has rounded leaves whose form resemble that of an ear. It branches out rapidly and its foliage provides excellent ground cover.

During flowering, it is covered with numerous green and red flowers. This perennial is found growing wild in the northern regions of France. In the garden it prefers limy soil and shady areas. It has an intense and unpleasant scent, similar to that of turpentine. Due to the asaron essential oil it contains, it has a bitter peppery taste. Its flowers can be harvested all year round.

In medicine, **wild ginger** was used as an emetic. In former times, drunkards used to consume the herb in

Wild ginger
Its fresh and dried leaves are used primarily to season white meats, fish and game.

order to empty their stomachs and sober up more quickly. This herb must be used with care because it can be toxic when consumed in high dosages. Craftsmen treasure it, because from it they can obtain an apple green color to dye wool.

BIXA ORELLANA   *Annatto*
Family: Bixaceae
Origin: Central America, the Caribbean
Height: 26 feet (8 m)
Flowering: summer
Properties: anti-inflammatory, febrifuge, relieves headaches, vermifuge

---

In the wild, the **annatto** is an average sized tree whose young branches are covered by soft, fine reddish hair while the older ones are smooth. Its large green leaves, which stand in long branches distributed alternately on the shoot, are covered with reddish stains on their underside.

The **annatto** flowers have a bright red color reminiscent of that of wild roses. They appear in terminal clusters of up to 20 flowers. Each flower consists of five big petals of up to 1.18 inches (3 cm) in diameter and several stamens. They produce heart shaped, bristly haired capsules which gradually fade from red into a brownish red color. Once they have matured in full, they burst releasing about 50 seeds.

In some developing countries, the **annatto** pigment has become an important export product. In order to obtain the pigment, the ripe fruit is harvested and soaked for some weeks in water to remove the coloring substance. This water is filtered, thickened, and dried in the air so as to form a reddish greasy, sticky paste.

The brick-red seeds, which have a peppery fragrance resembling that of **nutmeg**, are equally used themselves. Because they contain pigments such as norbixin, soluble in water, and bixin, soluble in fat, they can be used in a great number of ways.

Annatto has medicinal properties because it contains pigments, mineral salts, resins, flavonoid and salicylic derivatives. An infusion with the leaves and roots of this plant is used as a remedy for headaches.

Annatto is also used to lower fever and to fight dysentery. The husk of the seeds is used to fight worms. In Mexico and Paraguay, substances used in the treatment of cancer are extracted from it.

This natural dye is used in butter, chocolates, soups and cheese (Edamer, Red Leicester, Saint Paul, Chester). Even though it is used as a **saffron** substitute when cooking rice, it can never replace its aroma.

The seeds are also used to color oils. In industry, its water-soluble pigments are applied to lend a yellowish-orange tone to silk and wool. The red pigments under the effect of concentrated sulphuric acid give an indigo color.

Annatto is used to color lacquers, soaps and oils. Earlier, the plant was used by Central American Indians to paint their war masks with yellow-red colors. At the same time, South American natives colored their skin and hair with it. **Annatto** colorings are very beautiful, but ephemeral.

Mustard

As with cress, mustard leaves can be added to salads or can be cooked as a vegetable such as spinach (especially brown mustard leaves). They can also be pickled in vinegar and used as a relish. The whole seeds are used to season salads and pickled vegetables such as cucumbers. The difference between a hot and a mild mustard lies in whether the seeds are peeled (hot mustard) or unpeeled (mild mustard). Hot Dijon mustard goes very well with grilled meat and rabbit. It is also used as an ingredient in the preparation of certain mayonnaise recipes and is served with cold meat and sausages. Bordeaux mustard is a wonderful seasoning for sausages and cold meat; Beaujolais mustard fits perfectly to game. There are also the English mustards made from black and white mustard seeds, flour and turmeric. They have a very firm consistency and a shining yellow color. They are served with cooked meat. American mustards, sweetened and spiced, are made of white mustard seeds and turmeric. Such a mustard is inseparable from a Hot Dog. In a Vinaigrette, mustard may not be absent. Germinated seeds spice salads, raw fruits, and vegetable dishes.

BRASSICA ALBA, B. JUNCEA,	**Mustard**
B. NIGRA	

Family: *Cruciferae*
Origin: *Mediterranean washbasins (alba), China and India (juncea), Europe (nigra)*
Height: *11 to 15.7 inches (alba), 4.92 feet (juncea), 3.28 feet (nigra)*
Flowering: *according to sort from April to June*
Properties: *purgative (alba), balsamic, emetic (juncea and alba)*

Mustard is already mentioned in the Gospels of the New Testament. It was introduced to Spain by the Moors and spread from there all over Europe. It was first used as a medicinal plant. In the 13th century, the spicy taste obtained from crushing the seeds was discovered, and it began to be used as a spice.

The word **mustard**, which comes from *mostarde* (burning must) appeared for the first time in a text dating from 1288. Still today, many famous sorts of **mustard** come from France, predominantly from the regions around Dijon, Meaux, Bordeaux as well as from the Beaujolais. Since the 14th century, Dijon has been the world capital of **mustard** production; in 1382, the duke of Bourgogne, Philippe le Hardi, considered it one of his most valuable possessions.

There are three varieties of **mustard** seeds: **white**, **brown** and **black**. **Brown** and **black mustards** are very similar with a strong, pungent taste.

White mustard (*Brassica alba*) is an annual plant which is to be found wild on fallow land. It has

densely stemmed shoots with teethed light leaves. The yellow flowers have four petals and appear in terminal clusters. When they bloom they give way to hairy fruit and numerous siliques covered with pods containing anywhere between four and five yellowish-white seeds which have a pungent, sweet taste. In England, a seasoning is produced by combining this spice with **turmeric** (known under the code E 100).

The countries where **mustard** is grown are the United States, Canada, Great Britain, France, Denmark and the Netherlands. According to where it is cultivated, **brown mustard** (*Brassica juncea*) is also known as **Pakistan mustard** or **China mustard**. It was also found in Europe, mainly in Hungary and, later, in the 20th century in some regions of France (Gâtinais and Sologne).

The light green or dark green leaves of this plant grow mostly in rosettes. Seed pods, which remain closed after maturity preventing the seeds from falling to the ground, develop from the pale yellow flowers. The seeds have a light to dark brown color, a bitter pungent taste, and a weaker scent than that of **black mustard**. The closed siliques require, just like other **mustard** sorts, a mechanical harvest.

Brown mustard, one of the most popular varieties, is sown in the spring and harvested at the beginning of July.

The third variety is **black mustard** (*Brassica nigra*), a particularly undemanding plant. It has projecting stems and branches with roughly lobed leaves which become stronger at the ends. Its yellow flowers, appearing in terminal corymb clusters, develop pods containing dark brown seeds of strong, pungent taste.

Mustard seeds are widely used. However, its leaves are also consumed in salads or as a leafy vegetable. Among other things, the plant contains slime, alkaloids and enzymes. In moderate amounts, **mustard** stimulates the digestive system. It is used in compresses to alleviate bronchitis, lung diseases and congestion.

To produce **mustard**, the seeds are crushed with some water, which causes a chemical reaction that gives the mixture a sour, pungent taste. In order to halt this process, an acid like vinegar, wine or **lemon** juice is added. Most **mustard** recipes are prepared in this way.

Dijon mustard, which has a soft, creamy consistency, is made of ground **mustard** seeds, white wine, **salt** and **pepper**.

Beaujolais mustard, which is rougher, lumpier and slightly red, is made of coarsely crushed **mustard** seeds and red wine. **Meaux mustard** is also produced in this way, but it is milder, sweeter, and fairly grainy.

Bordeaux mustard, a mixture of **white** and **black mustard**, is made from unpeeled **mustard** seeds with sugar, vinegar, tarragon and other spices. It has a dark color and a sweet taste.

Red mustard is produced using whole grains and red **peppers**. Herbs and spice **mustard**, is made by mixing the ground grains with different spices or herbs.

CAPPARIS SPINOSA — Caper bush

Family: Capparidaceae
Origin: Asia
Height: 4 feet (1.2 m)
Flowering: spring
Properties: antispasmodic, apéritif, astringent, diuretic, stimulant, tonic

---

Caper bush

Capers are used to prepare white sauces. Finely chopped, they are an ingredient for tartar sauce and traditional rémoulade. They are used as a relish with fish, cooked veal, and as a seasoning for hors d'œuvres, salads and pizza.

The **caper bush** is a shrubby tree which is found wild in Europe all around the Mediterranean. Its flower buds – the **capers** – are usually pickled in vinegar. Although highly esteemed among the Greeks and the Romans, they made their appearance in Central Europe only after the 15th century.

The **caper bush** has numerous, very wide and branched out shoots with a smooth bark and dense, relatively firm, round leaves. It has beautiful big flowers with a white corolla and numerous high rising stamens.

Its fruit, which is generally cooked or pickled, is fleshy, green, oval and the size of an olive. It should,

however, not be confused with the immature flower buds of the shrub, also known as **capers**.

In warm, dry climatic regions, the **caper bush** is cultivated in open fields on light soil. The buds are harvested by hand every day of the blooming period. Afterwards, they are preserved in vinegar, brine or olive oil.

In order for them not lose their aroma, they have to be bathed in the liquid used to prepare them. They have a salty, sour taste. When fresh and unpickled, they contain a high degree of flavonoid used in the treatment of artherosclorosis. The bark also has medicinal purposes.

As a substitute to **capers** and also pickled in vinegar, immature harvested seeds of the indian cress or flower buds of the dandelion are sometimes used.

CAPSICUM ANNUUM	Bell pepper

Family: Solanaceae
Origin: South America, Central Asia
Height: 31.4 inches (80 cm)
Flowering: summer
Properties: apéritif, digestive, carminative, sudorific

This annual plant, used by native Americans as a medicinal plant, was discovered by **Christopher Columbus**. It was first introduced to Europe by the Spaniards in the 15th and 16th centuries from where it spread on to Africa, India and the Far East. Today, the different fruits of this plant have become worldwide spices.

There are more than 200 different **bell pepper** varieties whose fruit differ substantially in size, color, shape and taste. They can be long, small, rounded, thin, sweet or hot, and come in green, red, orange, purple, yellow, dark brown and black colors.

This herbaceous plant has branched, woody stems equipped with simple leaves that alternate in gentle colors of green. Its white, self-pollinating flowers bear generally elongated or rounded fruits which are green at first, gradually turning red, orange, yellow, purple or black once they have reached full maturity.

The fruit appears in the shape of big smooth, inflated, round or elongated berries. Their interior is formed by lobes which enclose numerous seeds. Their skin is hard, smooth and glossy. Their thick, juicy, sweet or pungent pulp is endowed with a gamut of different flavors.

The **bell pepper** is generally harvested by hand. It can be used either fresh, to be consumed raw and in the preparation of pastes and sauces, or else dried in the sun to preserve it or to obtain a powder. The plants are grown from seed on rich, humid soil and in sunny fields. Three months after sowing, the first fruits can be harvested.

The pungent taste of the **bell pepper** is due to capsaicin, which in great amounts can cause inflammation of the stomach and of the intestinal tract. Even though the **bell pepper** has a low nutritional value, it possesses medical properties.

Because it is rich in vitamin C, it has a tonifying effect, it stimulates the appetite and facilitates digestion of starchy foods. Furthermore, it improves blood circulation and promotes transpiration thereby having a cooling effect on the body.

Bell pepper

Bell peppers can be stuffed. They can also be used to flavor oils and vinegar, and to prepare spicy pastes with or without garlic and other aromatics like North African harissa. The fresh and dried fruit is used in the preparation of rice, white and red beans, pastes, and curry mixtures. Tabasco is made using hot chili peppers, sugar salt, and vinegar. Usually, a few drops are enough to strongly spice meat, eggs and cocktails.

When using this plant for culinary purposes, one can find all sorts of **bell peppers**: the **serrano pepper**, green or red, pungent and sweet; **cayenne pepper** (*Capsicum frutescens*), a small, thin, long, very strong, burning **pepper** which needs to be handled with care; **anaheim pepper**, green or red, thin, very sweet; **chili pepper**, green, red or orange, and especially strong. There are also the dry **Mexican peppers**.

Ancho chili, short, stocky fruity and sweet; **mulato chili**, similar to the previous one, but with a bit of a smoky taste; **tepin chili**, very small, rounded, sweet, with a bitter walnutty taste; **pasado chili**, used in soups and ragouts, when peeled tastes like a mixture of celery, apple and **lemon**; **cascabel chili**, also used in soups and ragouts, has a hazelnut taste; **guajillo chili**, sweet and tasting like green tea.

Among the **Spanish peppers** there are: the **guidilla**, very strong, but sweet, used in omelette's and with fish; **choricero chili**, a mild sort which is used in stews, salads and sausages. In France, in the Basque Provinces, the **espelette**-pepper is quite popular due to its incomparable taste and its gentle sweet, fruity aroma.

In the pharmaceutical industry, the **bell pepper** is used in the production of thermal cotton wool. The food industry uses an ethereal oil extracted from the fruit for the production of beverages.

CAPSICUM TETRAGONUM　　　*Paprika*

Family: *Solanaceae*
Origin: *Southern Mexico*
Height: *15.7 31.4 inches (40 to 80 cm)*
Flowering: *spring*
Properties: *apéritif, fortifier, tonic*

Paprika is the spicy powder obtained from a **bell pepper** variety found in Hungary. This plant was first introduced to Spain and Morocco and, later, around 1585 it arrived in Hungary. Although belonging to the same family (*Capsicum*) as **chiles** and **peppers**, this mild sort has established itself almost exclusively in Hungary. It owes its taste essentially to the sandy grounds and the climate.

By improving cultivation conditions, five different sorts have been developed of which the most well known are Kolocsa and Szeged. Similar varieties also grow in Mexico, India, in the former Yugoslavia, and in the Ivory Coast. In Spain there is also a variety known as pimiento whose only thing in common with a **pepper** is its name.

This half shrub has simple alternate leaves in shades of green. Its stems are woody and ramified and its white flowers are self-pollinating. They render inflated green berries that can reach up to 7.8 inches (20 cm) in length and become red when ripe. The interior of each berry is formed by lobes which enclose numerous seeds. Its skin is hard, smooth and glossy and it is thick and juicy.

The tangy fragrance of the fruits lies between that of a strong **chile** and a common sweet **bell pepper**. Because the plants are sensitive to temperatures under 50 °F (10 °C), they are sown once winter is over on nourishing soil. When the plant has sprouted and it begins to bloom, it is propped. Growth is slow requiring a lot of warmth, plenty of water and a rich soil.

Harvesting is done by hand from June to autumn. Afterwards, the fruits are put to dry. Once they are dry, the **paprika** is ground and turned into the powder we all know.

Paprika is the richest vegetable in vitamin C. This vitamin was isolated for the first time in 1933 by the Hungarian **Szent Gyorgiy**. Thanks to its high vitamin content, **paprika** is used to fight tiredness and stress, and is recommended as a reconstituent. It stimulates the appetite and the production of gastric juices. Due to its high content of vitamin A, it has an important role in the growth of children.

Ripe **paprika** contains carotene, a substance that adds a reddish color to dishes which are seasoned with this tasty spice.

Paprika

Dried, ground powdered paprika lends a gentle red coloring and a pungent, bitter-sweet taste to ragouts, game, fish, and vegetables. It is found raw in stuffed olives and as an ingredient in salads and stews. It can also be pickled in vinegar or oil and served as a spicy relish. And, of course, let's not forget that it is the most important ingredient in the Hungarian goulash.

CARICA PAPAYA   *Papaya*

Family: Caricaceae
Origin: Tropics
Height: 19.6 to 26.2 feet (6 to 8 m)
Flowering: spring
Properties: anti-inflammatory, carminative, laxative, digestive, vermifuge

Papaya was already cultivated in pre-Columbian times by the natives of Central America and Brazil. However, it was not until the 18th century that it made its appearance in Asia. Since then, it has been grown in tropical and subtropical regions.

This fast growing tree has a straight grey-green barked trunk with triangular stigma left by dead leaves. The plant is crowned by a bouquet of very big, terminal, seven lobed leaves with a long palmlike petiole. The **papaya** tree is generally dioecious: male and female flowers are produced by different plants. Male flowers, which are funnel-shaped, are borne in clusters on stalks placed on the leaf axils.

The female flowers are considerably larger, forked on very short stalks, and have a yellowish-white color. However, it can also be hermaphrodite, which is true of the solo variety, one of the most exported types because it is easily grown.

The size and weight of the fruit vary according to the species: they can be spherical or cylindrical and can weigh anywhere between 11 and 22 pounds, in some cases even more.

The pulp is whitish, red orange, or deep yellow and has the consistency of butter. The grey-black seeds, attached along the walls of the central cavity, are as big as **peppercorns** and have a taste reminiscent of that of cress or **mustard**.

These corns are gathered and used, fresh or dried, as a spice. **Papaya** is usually grown from seed and sown in April: the germinated plants are replanted on a rich, well drained soil in a warm, sunny location.

If the variety planted is dioecious, in order to guarantee the pollination and with it a rich yield of fruit, 20 female trees are planted for every male tree. At the end of the first season, the plants render the first fruit. Altogether, a plant yields fruit for up to five years.

The milky juice of the plant which is found in the leaves, the fruit and the seeds, contain papain, a vegetable enzyme. This proteolytic enzyme also supports the digestion of pectins, as well as of sugar, and lipids. Its function resembles that of similar enzymes found in the digestive tube.

It is used as a treatment for bile and liver ailments, as well as an aid to help digest protein and fat, and against bloating. In India, the seeds are chewed as a breath refresher and to facilitate digestion.

Papain helps eliminate adipose tissue, cellulitis, and because of its anti-inflammatory quality, it alleviates edema and haemorrhoids. It is also an excellent teeth cleanser and its corns are well known to kill amoebas and other intestinal parasites. To alleviate joint pain, bruises, and infected wounds, warm **papaya** leaves are applied directly to the skin.

Papain is used as a stabilizer when brewing beer and in the textile industry, it is applied to treat silk and wool, making them unshrinkable. In the tannery, it is used to cure leather. Among certain ethnic groups in Australia, it is consider an aphrodisiac.

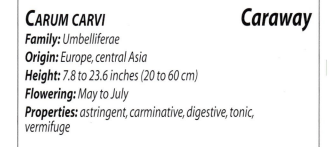

CARUM AJOWAN — Ajowan

Family: Umbelliferae
Origin: Southern India
Height: 15.7 to 23.6 inches (40 to 60 cm)
Flowering: summer
Properties: antiseptic, sedative, carminative, digestive, germicide

Ajowan resembles wild parsley. This annual plant grows in south India, Pakistan, Afghanistan, Iran and Egypt. Its flowers are arranged in umbels on long stems which, upon maturity, give way to the seeds.

Used as a spice, the seeds have an intense taste similar to that of thyme. **Ajowan** is grown in deep, nourishing, damp soil in a half-shady location. From the bitter, pungent seeds, an essential oil, known as thymol, is produced.

For centuries, **ajowan** has been used in India because of its medical properties: it alleviates asthma, diarrhoea, and indigestion. The ground seeds are used in cooking starchy foods to avoid flatulence. It is also used in pastries and in bread doughs (such as, nam, pakora and parata).

CARUM CARVI — Caraway

Family: Umbelliferae
Origin: Europe, central Asia
Height: 7.8 to 23.6 inches (20 to 60 cm)
Flowering: May to July
Properties: astringent, carminative, digestive, tonic, vermifuge

The **caraway** is one of the oldest known spices: it can be traced as far back as the Neolithic period. The Romans used it to flavor bread and extended their usage throughout the Empire.

In the Middle Ages, the plant was known as the so-called *carvi* and was used in love potions to ensure faithfulness.

Caraway grows wild in Europe, Siberia and in the Caucasus. The plant has spread throughout all continents settling in meadows, fallow land, mountain roads.

Papaya

Papaya seeds can be used as a spice in various ways. It contains the papain enzyme which is used in the manufacture of meat tenderizers. When used as a spice, it gives food a pungent, musky tang similar to that of cress. The crushed seeds can be added to meatballs, and can be used to spice grilled meat. It is also suitable when preparing marinades, game, and cream cheese. Its aroma goes well with sauces made to accompany fish.

In former times, the fruit of the wild plants were harvested. Today, instead, **caraway** is grown everywhere in heavy and humid ground.

Nevertheless, the seeds of wild **caraway** still have a more intense aroma. Countries where **caraway** is grown are the Netherlands, which produces the best quality seeds, followed by Germany, Poland, Scandinavia and Morocco.

This biennial plant belongs to the same family as the **carrot**. Its stem, which develops during the second year, is lightly branched, hollow and channelled. It has finely cut leaves that are smaller than the basal ones.

The small white flowers appear clustered in umbels. Its elongated, oval, brown fruit is a crescent often split in the bottom. In summer, the seeds are ripe and can be harvested.

Its spicy scent is very aromatic and its taste is reminiscent of **fennel** and **aniseed** with a pungent touch of **eucalyptus**.

The fruit has an aromatic essence composed mainly of carvon and limonene. It also contains tannin, proteins, oils, and flavonoid. The leaves contain carotene and vitamin C.

Caraway, with its pleasant aroma, is used to spice different foods. The finely chopped leaves are used in the preparation of soups, omelettes, and salads. It has a positive effect on the digestive system, preventing flatulence, fighting colic and facilitating digestion.

Caraway plays an important role in the flavoring of alcoholic beverages. It is used, for example, in aquavit, very popular in Scandinavian countries, gin and schnapps. Because of its aromatic properties, it is used in toothpaste and mouthwash.

CARYOTA URENS   ***Toddy palm***
Family: *Arecoideae*
Origin: *India, Malaysia, Sri Lanka and Burma*
Height: *65.6 feet (20 m)*
Flowering: *summer*
Properties: *nutritious, stimulant, tonic*

The **toddy palm** is a magnificent tree with a ringed trunk surmounted by a crown of approximately 15 long and large, featherlike bipinnate leaves which can be up to 20 feet long and 10 feet wide.

Its leaflets are pleated in a V-shape and have marginal teeth. Its flowers only bloom after 13 years with inflorescences developing just below the top of the trunk and appearing during the fifth year. Once the last flower has yielded the last fruit, the tree dies.

The round fruit, the size of a cherry, have a thin, firm skin of reddish-brown coloring and contain oxalate which makes them toxic.

However, the juice of **toddy palm** is used in the production of high-quality palm sugar, as well as palm wine. Because palm sugar consists of water, saccharose, and mineral salts, it is used to fight fatigue.

The juice of the **toddy palm** is also used like any other sugar to sweeten food and beverages, in jams and pastries.

The wood of the trunk is used in the manufacturing of slats and scaffolding. The pith of the trunk is used to make **sago**, and the dark fibers to make baskets, ropes and brushes.

CASSIA FISTULA   ***Cassia***
Family: *Caesalpiniaceae*
Origin: *Warm regions*
Height: *65.6 feet (20 m)*
Flowering: *March to May*
Properties: *laxative, nutritious, refreshing*

Cassia, a leguminous, is to be found in the dry regions of India and Sri Lanka.

There are many, very different kinds of **cassia** all over the world. Some are considered ornamental trees or shrubs.

Long, pale yellow or golden yellow clusters of hanging flowers make their appearance in early summer. The leaves, which can be up to 20 inches (50 cm) long, are pinnate, elongated, with a single oval, and leaflets measuring up to 7.8 inches (20 cm) long. Leaves remain on the tree for many months at a time.

The fruit, which can be almost as long as the leaves, resemble elongated, cylindrical **cloves** in dark, reddish brown. They are divided in several segments containing a black, sugary, sticky pith that holds the seeds.

This pith has a sweet, gentle taste and is used for its medical properties. The leaves are used for tea preparations as a purifier.

Caraway
Caraway has a pleasant scent and is used to spice sausages, meat dishes, especially goulash, bread, fermented cheeses like Munster cheese, salty biscuits, champignons, stews, sauces and vegetables (particularly, cabbage). Its finely chopped leaves are used in the preparation of herbal soups, salads, omelettes and potatoes.

**CHASMANTHERA PALMATA,
C. COLUMBA**

Calumba

Family: Menispermaceae
Origin: Africa
Height: 32 feet (10 m)
Flowering: spring
Properties: apéritif, stomachic, tonic

This perennial climber has aerial stems that wrap themselves around trees all the way to their top. Its lightly lobed leaves have long petioles and palmate veins. The white flowers, arranged in loose clusters, carry numerous, long stamens. The root of the plant is fleshy and can reach a diameter of 2.7 inches.

In Africa, it is one of the most important remedies for dysentery. **Calumba** was introduced to Europe in the 17th century by Portuguese sailors.

Composed of alkaloids and bitter substances, the **calumba** root is used to give aroma to apéritifs. It is also used in African and Asian cuisines to flavor dishes.

There is a variety, *Menispermium columba*, which is a half native of Sri Lanka. Its yellowish-green, bitter tasting root has drawn concentric circles, and is used to strengthen the stomach, to stimulate the appetite and during convalescence.

**CINCHONA LANCIFOLIA,
C. OFFICINALE,
C. SUCCIRUBRA**

**Cinchona
or China bark**

Family: Rubiaceae
Origin: Tropical America
Height: 98 feet (30 m)
Flowering: late spring
Properties: analgesic, apéritif, astringent, bactericide, cardiovascular regulator, febrifuge tonic

Cassia

The cassia pith is used to prepare delicious compotes, fruit pastes and other delicacies. It is also an ingredient for sweet and sour sauces. It can also be enjoyed at breakfast spread on a slice of toast or simply as a snack.

China bark is used to obtain a substance known as quinine.

It was only in the 17th century that Europeans living in Peru discovered the important medical properties of this plant. In 1648, it was brought to Europe for the first time by the **Countess of Chincon**, wife of the viceroy in Lima.

In France, the plant became popular once **Louis XIV.** began to use it in 1676. **Condamine**, the first sample of grey **cinchona** (*Cinchona officinale*) made it to Europe in the 18th century. The powder extracted from the bark of the tree was used to lower fever and in the treatment of malaria, a disease which caused tremendous devastation not only in tropical areas, but also in Europe.

In 1820, **Pelletier** and **Caventou** isolated from the bark of the plant the alkaloids quinine and quinidine.

Quinine soon replaced pulverized **china bark** in the treatment of many diseases.

The two most popular species are *C. officinale* which has a yellow bark, and *C. succirubra* which is rich in alkaloids. The latter sort supplies 90% of the world consumption of **china bark**.

Three sorts of **china bark** are currently in use. The **yellow bark**, the most popular one, *C. lancifolia*, is quite bitter. It is used to lower fever and yields 1.12 oz. of quinine from 2.2 lbs. of bark. The **grey bark**, derived from of *C. condamina* and *C. officinale*, also containing quinine, is bitter and is used as an astringent. **Red china bark**, *C. succirubra*, has a bitter and sour taste, but its quinine and quinidine counts are quite low. These trees are spread on the slopes of the Andes, mainly in high altitude forests with a humid, misty climate. They are evergreens with big, lancelike to oval, alternate, tough leaves.

The pink or creamy white flowers appear in big, terminal clusters. They produce small fruit similar to capsules with two veined, round or elongated chambers crowned by the calyx and containing numerous seeds. The flowers of the *C. succirubra* variety have a bright red color.

The bark of the trunk, the branches, and the roots of this variety of tree is used to produce quinine. Trees are grown in high altitudes of tropical, humid regions, and are rotated every 10 to 15 years.

Along with quinine and quinidine, **china bark** contains a few other alkaloids which are used to treat influenza, to lower fever, during convalescence, and against malaria.

Qunidine is an important alkaloid used to treat a variety of disorders of cardiac rhythm.

China bark is also used to stimulate the appetite by increasing the production of salivary and gastric secretions.

China bark is also used in the production of spirits, bitter beverages like tonic water, and in very sweet liqueurs with a particularly bitter taste used as apéritifs, such as Quinquina or Dubonnet.

CINNAMOMUM CAMPHORA　　**Camphor**
Family: Lauraceae
Origin: South China, Taiwan and Japan
Height: 49.2 feet (15 m)
Flowering: summer
Properties: antiseptic, cardio-stimulant, insecticide

Camphor is an aromatic tree from which an oil is extracted. It has been known for centuries in China and Japan where it is highly revered.

It is considered as a tree of life, because it can grow to be enormous and can reach a very old age (several centuries, in some cases up to 1,000 years). In the Chinese mythology, it is said that if upon entering paradise one is offered its fruit, immortality is being granted.

In the 12th century, while trading with the Far East, the Arabs discovered this medicinal plant which they later brought to Europe. The use of **camphor** became wide spread during the 17th century.

Camphor

In medicine, camphor is applied externally as a decongestant and used internally as a heart stimulant. It is found as an ingredient in balms used against aching muscles and rheumatic pain. It is used to disinfect contaminated areas and it is a good natural insecticide.

Camphor is a strong, evergreen tree. It has a knotty trunk and a rich foliage. Its smooth, glossy leaves are oblong with a long petiole.

When young, they are red, but, with time, they become green and glossy with a bluish green underside. Its small, yellowish flowers are arranged in loose inflorescences which give way to the dark purple single seeded fruit.

The fragrance of **camphor** is very strong and it has a bitter, aromatic taste.

The tree begins to produce **camphor** after 25 years and only when it is 40 does it reach its production climax. It is then that the tree is cut down and its wood chopped to extract **camphor**. Trees found in Sumatra and Borneo sometimes grow to an enormous height, often over 100 ft.

Volatile and lighter than water, **camphor** is used in a number of different industrial ways; it is mostly used in the manufacturing of lacquers. Modern applications include the use of **camphor** as a plasticizer for cellulose nitrate, as a flavoring, and in fireworks.

Many essential oils, such as those of lavender, rosemary, marjoram, balk fern and valerian contain **camphor** in small amounts.

CINNAMOMUM CASSIA — Chinese cinnamon

Family: *Lauraceae*
Origin: *Burma*
Height: *9.8 feet (3 m)*
Flowering: *summer*
Properties: *carminative, fortifier, tonic*

Chinese cinnamon has been used for centuries in China and Egypt to season food and in order to embalm the dead. It is mentioned in the Bible. **Chinese cinnamon** is the most well known **cinnamon** in the world.

Today, the plant is cultivated predominantly in China, South-East Asia and Central America. The spice is obtained by peeling the bark from stems and branches and setting it aside to dry in the sun. While drying, the bark curls into quills.

Chinese cinnamon is a tree that grows in all tropical regions. Its foliage resembles that of bay leaf. The fruit, which looks like a **clove**, develops out of the yellow flowers. It is rich in essential oils and is used to relieve flatulence and digestive disorders. At the same time, it is recommended during a child's development and during convalescence.

Chinese bark is an ingredient present in meat curries, the Chinese five spice powder, and vegetables pickled in vinegar. It goes well with fruit compotes and is used to add fragrance to chocolate.

Even though **Chinese** and **Ceylon cinnamon** belong to the same family, they yield very different spices.

Cinnamon

Cinnamon, with its exotic, sugary aroma and its sweet taste, is used to enhance savory and sweet dishes alike. Generally, it is found in powder or in small sticks. It is used ground to flavor cakes, pastries and biscuits. Cinnamon sticks spice ragouts, rice, mulled wines, punch and fruit syrups. It is the spice of choice for Moroccan tajine and Iranian rice. It is an ingredient in the so called five spice powder. In Germany and Russia it is used to add aroma to chocolate. With the dried flower buds one can prepare a fragrant musky infusion.

CINNAMOMUM ZEYLANICUM — Ceylon cinnamon

Family: *Lauraceae*
Origin: *Sri Lanka*
Height: *23 to 32.8 feet (7 to 10 m)*
Flowering: *summer*
Properties: *antiseptic, antispasmodic, astringent, carminative, febrifuge, stimulant*

The spice is an extract taken from the bark of a tree native to the island of Sri Lanka, known as **Ceylon cinnamon** (*Cinnamomum zeylanicum*). Regarded as the "real" **cinnamon** plant, it produces a very high quality **cinnamon** which is quite popular in Europe because of its delicate aroma. This **cinnamon** is one of the oldest and most precious spices.

The Egyptians already sought it to elaborate perfumes and to embalm the dead. In the Bible, (Exodus 30:29), it is mentioned as being more precious than gold.

Real **Ceylon cinnamon** is grown in different tropical countries: Sri Lanka, Madagascar, Brazil and on the Seychelles. **Ceylon cinnamon** is a small tree with a reddish, aromatic bark. Its evergreen leaves are rough,

plain and glossy with an elongated, oval shape. When young, they are red. As they age, however, they turn dark green. The pale yellow flowers stand in clusters producing round, green to dark reddish brown, pearlike, large fruit.

The **Ceylon cinnamon** tree is cultivated in sandy ground and in humid, warm regions. Under optimal conditions, eight to ten shoots are formed at the foot of the plant, which are cut every three years. The crop is harvested in the wet season to facilitate the removal of the bark. The shoots are scraped and rubbed to loosen the bark which is split and peeled. While drying, the bark curls into quills forming the **cinnamon** sticks and acquires its color.

Ceylon cinnamon contains various essential oils, cinnamic aldehyde, mucus, and tannin. It is used against upset stomach, diarrhoea, and intestinal problems. Its essential oil, produced through the distillation of the leaves, contains up to 70% of eugenol. It is used as a cough suppressant, to relieve fever, colds, and rheumatic and muscle pain. It also serves as a substitute for **clove** oil.

CITRUS AMBLICARPA,	**Wild lemon,**
C. HYSTRIX	**Combava**

Family: *Rutaceae*
Origin: *Far East, Thailand*
Height: *13 to 16.4 feet (4 to 5 m)*
Flowering: *April / May until autumn*
Properties: *apéritif, tonic*

This **citrus fruit** is a wild or half **wild lemon**. Like other **citrus fruits**, **wild lemon** grows in warm, tropical regions. The shrub, strongly reinforced with thorns, grows somewhat sparingly and has a very dense foliage. The fruit resembles a very small green **lemon** with an irregularly dented outer rind. It is used mainly as a spice since it produces very little juice. Its greenish pith has a very sour, bitter taste. When ripe, the thick and crumbled rind has a yellow color. However, the fruit is regularly harvested early when it is still green because it contains a greater amount of essential oils.

The dark, plain green leaves of the shrub are grouped in pairs and have a typical winged petiole. Their fragrance is a bit bitter. The fruit, with its thick, porous skin and its round shape ending in a broad apical nipple, has a very rough appearance. Because it contains essential oils and vitamin C, **wild lemon** juice is used in the production of shampoos, creams, and tonics.

Wild lemon

Its rough leaves are used to flavor Indonesian and Thai dishes. They are also suitable to give aroma to mild sauces, fish and poultry, soups and curries. Occasionally, the juice is used in cocktails as a substitute for lemon juice. Its aromatic zest is used to make perfumes. Fresh and dried wild lemon leaves are readily available in Asian grocery shops. The fresh leaves can be kept frozen.

CITRUS AURANTIIFOLIA	**Lime**

Family: *Rutaceae*
Origin: *South East Asia*
Height: *13 to 16.4 feet (4 to 5 m)*
Flowering: *spring to autumn*
Properties: *anti-rheumatic, antiscurvy, antiseptic, febrifuge, refreshing, mineralizer, tonic*

Lime, also known as **sour lime** or **green lemon**, is a **citrus fruit** which is frequently found in South America and Asia. The tree was brought to the Mediterranean region by the Crusaders. It was not until three centuries later, in the 16th century, that the Portuguese planted these trees in Central and South America where they are grown.

Today, the most well known varieties are: the varieties from Mexico and the Antilles, which have a round fruit and a dark green rind; those from Tahiti and Persia, which are bigger, seedless, more juicy and less acid; and the **Rangpur limes**, which are intensely fragrant.

The plant is a small tree which is strongly reinforced with thorns and a very dense foliage. It grows in tropical warm regions. The fruits have a relatively thin outer rind and are formed by a zest, containing a very aromatic essential oil, and an indigestible white spongy mesocarp or albedo – the inner part of the peel.

The juicy, acid pulp is segmented into several portions containing the seeds. Rich in vitamin C, **lime** contains few calories. It has trace elements, mineral salts, pectin, sugar, as well as maleic and citric acid. **Limes** were formerly used in the British Navy to prevent scurvy; hence the nickname "Limey."

Lime is frequently mistaken with **green lemon**. However, they are two different fruits. While the rind of the **lime** is thin, that of the **green lemon** is very thick and has a characteristic, sour scent. **Lime** gives a sustained bitter aroma to certain soft drinks. It is also used to splash dishes with an acidy taste. Compared to **wild lemons**, **limes** are more juicy.

In Indonesian and Thai dishes , its ground leaves and rind are used as an aromatic spice. It is used to season pork, game and fish, like the Mexican ceviche (raw fish marinated in **lime** juice), salads, and desserts. Its finely chopped leaves are added to soups and curries. In addition, its zest is used to spice punch.

From a more practical point of view, **lime** juice diluted in water is used to rinse, perfume and make hair shiny; for this reason, it is used in the manufacturing of shampoos. Its juice is used to prepare creams and, in Malaysia, to prepare fortifying tonics.

CITRUS AURANTIUM	**Sour**
	or Seville orange

Family: *Rutaceae*
Origin: *probably China and eastern India*
Height: *16.4 to 19.6 feet (5 to 6 m)*
Flowering: *from spring to autumn*
Properties: *antispasmodic, apéritif, tonic, stomachic, vermifuge*

The **Seville orange**, also known as **sour orange**, is a close relative of the **orange**. However, it differs from it because its pulp is at the same time sour and bitter. The **Seville orange** was the first **orange** to be introduced to Europe, mainly in Italy and Spain. Today, because of its sour taste, other sweeter **oranges** are preferred.

Closely related to **bergamot**, the **Seville orange** is a perennial thorn shrub with stalky rough, fragrant leaves. Its white flowers stand on relatively long stems producing the fruit or **oranges**. These are round, with a bitter and unedible pulp; however, their orange colored rind has a fragrant zest.

Seville oranges are grown in open fields, in the warm lands of the Mediterranean basin. They need a sandy and fertile soil that is well drained and is well irrigated during the summer months. The buds produced by the plants can be used in grafting. The fruits are harvested from November to March, when they are ripe.

The leaves and the bark of the **Seville orange**, rich in vitamin C and in neroli, an essential oil, are used in infusions to alleviate stomach aches, relieve cramps and fight against intestinal parasites.

A perfumed water used as a tonic is obtained from its flowers. In the south of France, as well as in South America, this essence is highly valued for its seasoning properties.

In the spirit industry, there are liqueurs which are produced using the bark of **Seville orange**: Curaçao and Cointreau. In perfumery, the particularly fragrant oil of the bark, the flowers and the leaves are used. The wood which has a bright yellow color, is very hard and has a nice shine; therefore, carpenters often use it.

Lemon

Lemon goes well with white meat, poultry and, of course, fish. Its juice spices vinaigrettes, mayonnaise and other sauces. The fruit can be prepared whole cured in a brine. Lemon is found in sorbets, pastries and different desserts, such as cakes, pies and tarts. Lemon soufflé is prepared using its zest and juice. Its aroma is used in confectionery. It is almost unconceivable to have a fish or seafood dish without lemon, even when some gourmands refuse to use it with sea urchins. Lemon is also used to prepare a bitter jam like the English marmalade.

CITRUS BERGAMIA **Bergamot**
Family: *Rutaceae*
Origin: *southern Italy (Calabria)*
Height: *16.4 to 29.5 feet (5 to 9 m)*
Flowering: *from late spring until autumn*
Properties: *antiseptic, antispasmodic, aromatic, sedative*

A close relative of the sweet **orange**, **bergamot** has a delicious strong scent. Today, in the Ivory Coast, this fruit tree is planted mainly for its aroma.

Its branches, sometimes thorny, have dark, glossy, oblong, green leaves with serrated edges and a relatively hard texture. Its white flowers release a delicate scent and produce yellow, pear shaped fruits which can reach an average of 2.7 to 3.9 inches in length.

Its zest contains 0.5% of essential oil giving the plant aromatic and therapeutic properties. It also serves as a photosensitizer thanks to the components found in its essential oil. It is used in perfumery, in confectionery, and in the production of liqueurs. It is an ingredient in the famous Eau de Cologne and in many tanning lotions

In England, it is used to give fragrance to different pastries and the well known Earl Grey tea. The plant and the bark are used to make sweets, also known as **bergamots**.

CITRUS LIMON **Lemon**
Family: *Rutaceae*
Origin: *India*
Height: *13.1 to 16.4 feet (4 to 5 m)*
Flowering: *from May until autumn*
Properties: *anti-rheumatic, antiseptic, purifier, diuretic, febrifuge, fungicide*

In the wild, **lemon** trees grow at the base of the Himalaya, more exactly in Nepal, Bhutan, India and Pakistan. The plant appeared first in Mesopotamia, and then spread to Egypt, Palestine and North Africa. During the Crusades, it arrived in Sicily. In the 16th century, it arrived in the New World and began to be grown in the Antilles.

Today, the **lemon** tree can be found in subtropical regions of the earth. It is a small, spreading tree with a grey bark. Its evergreen leaves are light green. Its sweetly perfumed flowers, which have petals that are white on top and purple below, are grouped in clusters on the axils of the leaves.

The **lemon** fruit is oval with a broad, low, apical nipple. When young, it is greenish brown; when ripe, it turns yellow.

The zest of the **lemon** possess a very aromatic essential oil. Like any other **citrus**, it is exceptionally rich in vitamin C and contains 5 to 10% of citric acid. So that its purifying property can be effective, one has to drink its juice freshly pressed, or apply it directly on the skin in a compress. Due to its acidity, in case of fever, a **lemon** infusion refreshes the body and helps against

cystitis. When taken in the early stages, **lemon** can help stop colds. Its zest is rubbed on the skin to treat fungal infections. It is also an antioxidant that prevents other fruits from turning black when cut.

In carpentry, its wood is frequently used. In the dyeing trade, **lemon** is used to obtain the red textile dye known as carthamin.

CITRUS MEDICA   *Citron*

Family: *Rutaceae*
Origin: *forests of the Himalaya, Indo-China*
Height: *9.8 to 13.1 feet (3 to 4 m)*
Flowering: *from April to autumn*
Properties: *antihaemorrhagic, antiscurvy, antiseptic, febrifuge, refreshing, tonic*

Citron resembles a big **lemon** and is very much appreciated because of its aroma. The plant has always been cultivated in India and China. The soldiers of Alexander the Great brought it to Europe along with the **sour orange**; both trees soon spread throughout the Mediterranean. Very quickly, the ancient Greeks and Romans came to appreciate it; evidence of this are the numerous Roman mosaics on which it is represented. In Rome, it was used as a fragrant condiment conserved in **salt**. Today, **citron** is grown in Italy between Genoa and Florence.

This evergreens tree is smaller than a **lemon** tree and carries short, rigid branches which are reinforced by thorns. Its pale green leaves are broadly oblong and slightly serrate. Its flowers, which have a purple or magenta color, are rather big and scarce. The fruit, is big with a thick, very irregular bark

At first, the fruit is red; when ripe, it turns green and later yellow. **Citron** has a less acid pulp and a weaker perfume than **lemon**. Its peel has a very fragrant essential oil that is highly valued.

Because **citron** contains citric and maleic acid, potassium, calcium, sugar, mineral salts, pectin, slime, trace elements and vitamin C, it has a number of medicinal properties; its essential oil, which is extracted from its rind, works as an effective antiseptic.

When cooking it, its crystallized peel is used to flavor pastries and prepare delicious marmalades. It is also used to make perfumes, eau de toilette, and several other beauty products.

There are several varieties of this plant: *the fruit of the Etrog* variety, used in the Jewish feast of *Soucoth* to make the ritual *loulab* bouquet; the *Citrus medica sacrodactylis* known in China as *hand of Buddha* because the fruits are arranged in the manner of hands folded for prayer. In the Japanese mythology, the fruit of this variety of tree, along with **pomegranates** and peaches, is considered to be one of the three plants that bring good luck.

CITRUS SINENSIS   *Sweet or Common orange*

Family: *Rutaceae*
Origin: *hybrid offsprings of the Seville orange*
Height: *39.3 feet (12 m)*
Flowering: *from spring to autumn*
Properties: *antiscurvy, antispasmodic, aperitif, diuretic, laxative, tonic*

The **orange** is the most well known **citrus fruit**. It has endured multiple transformations due to the fact that it has been crossbred several times. It was introduced to Spain by the Arabs and made its way into France through the Côtes de Provence.

It was under **François I**, that the first breed appeared, while **Louis XIV** promoted their cultivation and constructed the famous orangeries in Versailles. Today, **oranges** are grown in a number of tropical countries, the main producer being Brazil.

Oranges can be classified into three groups: navel **oranges**, which mature particularly early; light **oranges** like the **Maltese**, the **Jaffa** and the late **Valencia**; and **blood oranges**, which are harvested from January to March.

An **orange** tree has a life expectancy of 300 to 400 years. It has an elegant, round stature and carries evergreen, elongated, serrated leaves. Its white flowers, which have a very delicate perfume, contain the essential oil neroli.

The rounded fruit, or **oranges**, are divided inside in approximately ten segments containing a juicy pulp. The pulp is covered by a bark made of two layers: the exterior layer, or zest, is thin and contains a volatile, inflammable oil which, upon maturity of the fruit and according to the sort of **orange**, is colored orange, reddish or greenish orange; the white inside layer is thick

---

Sweet orange

Sweet orange is generally eaten raw, as a juice, or as a dessert. However, it is also used in recipes to prepare dishes like duck à l'orange, pork, chicken and veal. The whole fruit is used to prepare marmalades, cakes and sorbets. Its crystallized peel, is used as a decoration and in sweets; its zest is used in appetizers and pastries. Particularly delightful is the combination of crystallized orange peel with chocolate.

with a tough cotton wool consistency. **Oranges** are relatively easy to grow: they need a warm climate and thrive in almost any soil, as long as it is not too loamy. Consisting of 85% water, **oranges** are good thirst quenchers. They are rich in vitamin C and other vitamins such as vitamins A and B. They also contain mineral salts, especially calcium, and sugar.

In pharmaceutics, **orange** leaves are used because of their tonic and antispasmodic properties, and **orange** flowers are used for their sedative qualities. Neroli oil, which is distilled from the flowers, has an important role in the cosmetics and perfume industries. It is used, for example, in eau de toilette, soaps and bath essences. Its hard and compact wood is valued in carpentry. The orange flower symbolizes virginity; therefore, it is used in bridal bouquets.

CLEOME HASSERLIANA

Cleome or Spiderflower

Family: *Capparaceae*
Origin: *all tropical regions*
Height: *3.93 feet (1.2 m)*
Flowering: *late spring to midsummer*
Properties: *apéritif, stimulant, tonic, vermifuge*

In the warm regions of the earth, there are more than 200 different kinds of **cleome**. A close relative of the **caper** shrub, it too possesses medical properties.

This annual, herbaceous plant has a sticky appearance. Its alternating, featherlike leaves consist of three to seven leaflets with a thorny petiole. Its flowers, which appear alone or in terminal clusters have an intense fragrance, a dark pink to whitish color and projecting stamens. Its fruits look like husky capsules containing numerous seeds. Like **capers**, the flower buds of this plant are harvested when they reach the size of a pea. They are picked and left to wither for a day, before immersing them in brine, vinegar or oil.

The **cleome** contains essential oils, mineral salts, flavonoid and vitamins. It is used to stimulate the appetite, facilitate digestion and fight against intestinal parasites. Its pickled seeds are used as a spice to season sauces and vinaigrettes, in stuffings and in herb-flavored butter. It is used as a garnish for hors-d'œuvres and salads. The **cleome**, with its fragrant flowers, is also popular as a garden plant.

An orangery

COFFEA ARABICA

Coffee

Family: *Rutaceae*
Origin: *high plateau of Ethiopia*
Height: *32.8 feet (10 m); in cultivation limited to 16.4 feet (5 m)*
Flowering: *after the rainy season*
Properties: *aromatic, diuretic, stimulant, tonic*

The world's most favorite aromatic beverage is made from the seeds of this plant. It is believed that **coffee** was grown in the mountain regions of Yemen and the Arab countries already in the 15th century.

There are different stories about the discovery of the invigorating properties of **coffee**. Here we have chosen to honor that of an Arab shepherd. It is said that he noticed his goats were exceptionally lively after they had eaten the leaves and seeds of the **coffee** tree. Most probably the Arabs were the first to produce the beverage which, from 15th century on, spread throughout the East and conquered Europe only two centuries later. It is documented for the first time in Venice in 1615, and in 1654 in Marseilles. Thévenot introduced it to Paris in 1657, but it only came into fashion in 1669 with the Ottoman ambassador **Soliman-Aga.**

The Dutch were the first Europeans to cultivate the **coffee** tree on Java at the end of the 17th century. In 1714, a **coffee** tree was planted in the Jardin des Plantes in Paris, and in 1720 another plant arrived on Martinique. Soon its cultivation expanded throughout the Antilles, and in 1727, it began to be grown in Brazil, Jamaica and Cuba. At the time of the French revolution, France became the major **coffee** producer of the world.

The **coffee** tree is regularly trimmed to give it a robust framework and stimulate fruiting. It has long, pointed, rough, green leaves that are slightly waved at the edges. Its white flowers, grouped on the stems, give off a pleasant fragrance. Its fruit, bright red, fleshy berries, contain two flattened seeds (the **coffee** beans) opposite each other. This delicate half shrub requires a warm climate; it bears fruit only after three to five years. Its lifespan varies between 60 and 100 years. There are approximately 60 different **coffee** sorts which, depending on the plan of cultivation, have different qualities.

The seeds contain 1.5 to 2.5% of caffeine alkaloid, tannin, as well as a bitter aromatic oil with stimulating qualities. **Coffee** stimulates blood circulation and digestion. In former times, it was also given as an antidote for opium.

COLA ACCUMINATA	Cola
Family: Steriulaceae	
Origin: tropical Africa	
Height: 32.8 to 65.6 feet (10 to 20 m)	
Flowering: early summer	
Properties: astringent, stimulant	

The **cola** tree grows wild in tropical regions. It has oval, leathery, leaves with hermaphrodite or male only creamy, white flowers that stand in loose groups on older shoots. The fruit that develop from the flowers are called **cola** nuts. They have the size of chestnuts and their color can vary from yellow, to red or brown. Their taste is bitter and astringent.

Besides having starch, sugar, lipids and proteins, **cola** nuts contain alkaloids (caffeine and theobromine) to which they owe their stimulating effect on the muscle and nervous system. In pastry, they are used to flavor cookies. However, they owe their popularity to **Coca-cola**, the famous drink invented last century by an American pharmacist.

The coffee tree

Once the ripe fruit are harvested, the seeds are removed from their husks and left to dry. Afterwards they are roasted, developing their brown color and aroma. Today, coffee is one of the most popular beverages in the world. It is prepared in various ways: cappuccino, iced coffee, espresso etc. Furthermore, coffee aroma is used in pastry creams and also for ice cream. Taken in great amounts, it can cause sleeplessness and be harmful to the heart.

CORIANDRUM SATIVUM	Coriander
Family: Umbelliferae	
Origin: Asia Minor	
Height: 23.6 inches (60 cm)	
Flowering: summer	
Properties: antiseptic, antispasmodic, carminative, digestive, fortifier, stimulant	

Even though **coriander** is used rather rarely in western dishes, it is the most cultivated spice in the world. The plant is mentioned in the Bible as a bitter herb of Easter. **Coriander** seeds were also found in the Pharaohs tombs. The Romans introduced it to Europe. In the Middle Ages, it was also used against fleas.

This annual herb has a tap root and strongly branched out shoots which are covered with finely cut leaflets. The small, white or pink flowers stand in inflorescences in the form of umbrellas. Red-brownish seeds develop out of them. The leaves, which taste of **aniseed**, and the seeds, whose taste resembles that of orange peel, are the parts of the plant that are used. In Asia the root is also eaten as a vegetable.

Coriander is grown from seed in the spring on permeable ground in a sunny location. It grows quickly and the leaves can be harvested fresh during the whole season.

Coriander is an excellent medicinal plant: it stimulates the appetite and has an alleviating effect on flatulence, tiredness, cramps and arteriosclerosis. Besides, it possesses antiseptic qualities, facilitates digestion and is a component of the famous Carmelite spirit. The fresh plant is rich in vitamin A.

The seeds contain an essential oil, tannin, proteins, sugar and vitamin C. By distillation, an essence with pharmaceutical use can be obtained. An infusion made from its crushed seeds, enjoyed after a meal, eases digestion.

Coriander seeds are used as a spice. Its leaves are an ingredient in salads, soups and ragouts. They season vegetables, lamb, chicken, meatballs, sauces, fish and seafood.

Coriander should be added at the end of the cooking process because its aroma easily fades when heated. It stays fresh only a few days after it is cut, but can be kept frozen. The seeds are often found dried, whole or pulverized. They are a component of many spice mixtures, like curry powders, Indian garam

massala and ras-el-hanout from North Africa. They give aroma to marinades for meat and fish, broths, vegetable dishes, cooked fruit, as well as pickled cucumbers, and chutneys. Whole and ground, the seeds are used in Greek cuisine and in sweet and sour recipes. They are also used to give aroma to alcoholic drinks, sweet pastries and **gingerbread**.

Roasted, ground and then mixed with **cumin**, they yield an aromatic mixture which is popular in the Middle East. The essential oil of **coriander** is used in the production of soaps and some perfumes.

CORNUS MAS — Cornelian cherry

Family: Cornaceae
Origin: Caucasus, Turkey, warm regions of Central Europe
Height: 9.8 to 23 feet (3 to 7 m)
Flowering: in the spring, before the leaves sprout
Properties: antidiarrhoea, antispasmodic, purifier, tonic

Sumach is the name of the powder which is obtained from grinding the cherries of the male **cornelian cherry** plant.

This half shrub thrives in dry, hard ground and is found on fallow land, in forests and on rocky slopes. It has very hard wood and elliptic leaves arranged in opposing pairs with remarkable veins.

Its beautiful, small, yellow, hermaphrodite flowers, grouped in short umbels, produce lots of pollen and decorate the tree until the leaves sprout. During Flowering, it is beautiful; therefore, it is often found decorating gardens. Moreover, it is highly tolerant of frost. Its tasty fruit are oval, red with a yellow red pulp. Its taste is both acid and bitter.

The fruit are harvested in August and September when they are ripe, but still firm. They can be consumed fresh, or dried in the sun to make **sumach**.

The pulp is rich in vitamin C, pectin, maleic and tartaric acid, sugar, tannin, and several mineral salts. An infusion from **cornelian cherry** is a great tonic to be used during convalescence. The juice alleviates indigestion and strong diarrhoea in children. Its stone contains an oil which is used to alleviate stomach disorders and diarrhoea.

In the early days, a yellow color was produced out of the bark of **cornelian cherry** to dye wool, silk and cotton.

Cornelian cherry

Cornelian cherry fruit can be consumed fresh in compotes, as an addition to game or as a jam. It can be used to prepare wine, syrup and liqueurs. To produce the spice sumac, the fruits are dried, and ground into a powder. The spice is then kept in a sealed jar in a dark place. Its mildly sour taste goes well with soups, ragouts, sauces, some fish, grills, salads, apple purée and sweet creams.

CROCUS SATIVUS — Saffron

Family: Iridaceae
Origin: probably present-day Iraq
Height: 3.9 inches (10 cm)
Flowering: autumn
Properties: antispasmodic, emmenagogue, sedative, stimulant, tonic

---

This monocotyledon, bulbous, perennial also known as **crocus**, thrives in the wild on prairies and mountain meadows. The plant is cultivated for economic reasons in southern Europe (Spain, Italy and Greece). The main country of origin is, however, the United Arab Emirates.

During the crusades, the plant came to Europe and up to the 20th century, France was an important producer of **saffron**. Allegedly, its bulbs were brought into the country by **La Rochefoucauld** and the knight **d'Argence** hidden in a hollow reed.

In the 16th century considerable amounts were harvested in the Angoumois region. **Saffron** from Balzac, Champniers, Salles and Bayers were considered to be of higher quality. Around 1650, the cultivation in Champniers flourished, where a hall was especially built for this purpose. Around 1880, cultivation was reduced in favor of wine. This decline continued till 1918.

Today, **saffron** is still cultivated in Gâtinais and, since 1987, attempts to cultivate it have been made in Coutras, in the Gironde, in Fontenay sur Dive, in the Charente where **saffron** bulbs are set in truffle fields. This astute system allows for the cultivation of two precious products on a limited surface with a maximum profitability.

Saffron consists of a bulb which is surrounded by a fibrous membrane. It has thin, straight leaves which appear at the same time as the flowers. The relatively big flowers, which have an upright bell shape and are soft purple, open at night and close during the day. The feathery orange tip of the pistils is divided in three stigmas that contain a color. These stigmas are the ones to be dried and used as a spice.

When **saffron** is harvested, the stigmas are hand-picked from each flower. To prosper well, **saffron** needs a sandy ground and a sunny location.

Saffron is grown in tight, crowded groups of plants. It is the most expensive spice in the world due to the fact that to obtain less than an ounce of

saffron, approximately 140 to 160 flowers must be harvested. In other words, 2.2 lbs. of stigmas corresponds to the yield of 140,000 to 160,000 flowers.

In many countries, because it is so expensive, other coloring spices are used: **turmeric** in India, Sri Lanka and China; marigolds in Europe.

A plant which resembles **saffron** and also blooms in autumn is the colchicum commonly known as **meadow saffron**. It has a similar form, but rather pink flowers. It also belongs to the family of the lily plants and is highly poisonous.

In the Bible, it is named among the sweet smelling herbs in the Song of Solomon. In Greek-Roman mythology, Crocos is a very good young boy, but at the same time a mortal who dares to bother Smilax, the nymph. As a punishment for his impudence he was transformed into a **saffron** plant.

Saffron is reputed to be an aphrodisiac. The Egyptians brought it from Mesopotamia. **Pliny the Elder** remarked that nothing was falsified more often than this spice. Swindlers were strongly punished, sometimes even executed. The Phoenicians and later the Romans introduced **saffron** to Europe. It is said that Nero had the streets of Rome sprinkled with **saffron** when he made his entrance into the city.

The Romans used this spice to fight hangovers and coughs. In the Middle Ages, it was used during childbirth to soothe pain. Afterwards, the color of **saffron** became a symbol of the heart. In the Renaissance, it was used to attempt to fight the plague. This was without a doubt the reason why its cultivation increased during this period, although the spice was also used for culinary reasons.

In France, cultivation areas were concentrated in certain regions: around Albi and Angoulême, in the Gâtinais – with Boysne the world capital of **saffron** during these days – and in the region around Pacy-sur-Eure in Normandy. Later on, more reasonably priced substitutes came onto the market and its demand decreased. In the early 1940's, repeated strong frosts caused the plants to disappear completely in the most important cultivation areas.

Saffron has many medical properties. It facilitates sleep, alleviates flatulence and menstrual pain. Its stamens contain a volatile, aromatic essential oil containing a bitter hetorchain, rich in vitamin B2, which is responsible for the typical scent of **saffron**. The plant also has phytosterol, a vegetable hormone and other

alkaloids (picrocrocin). Its intense yellow-orange pigment gives the plant a great coloring power: it is used to give a golden tone to some liqueurs such as Chartreuse, and also to color textiles. In addition, it is this pigment which gives the characteristic tint to the garments of the Buddhist monks in Tibet. Because of its spicy smell **saffron** is also used in perfumery.

In the garden, **saffron** can be an ornamental plant; planted in tight groups, it produces a very decorative bunch of colors.

CUMINUM CYMINUM　　　　**Cumin**
Family: Umbelliferae
Origin: Mediterranean region, Asia Minor
Height: 9.8 inches (25 cm)
Flowering: spring
Properties: apéritif, carminative, digestive, galactagogue, sudorific

This ancient herb from Asia Minor was adopted by the Chinese, the Indonesians and later by the Indians. **Cumin** plays an important role in medicine and cookery. The Romans used it after huge banquets.

In the Middle Ages, it was popular not only for its medical properties, but also because it was believed to be a protection against witchcraft and evil spells. In the kitchen, it is often substituted by **caraway** which has a similar fruit, but a much stronger scent and a bitter, hot taste.

This annual tropical plant, which is cultivated in different countries, has finely dissected leaves and its small pink or white flowers are arranged in umbels. The flowers bear small, elongated seeds, lighter than those of **caraway**.

Cumin thrives in humid ground in sunny locations and is grown from seed. The seeds are harvested four months after being sowed when they are yellow, and then dried in the sun. In Iran, there is a variety, **black cumin**, which is milder with smaller, black seeds. **Cumin** has a strong, spicy and sweet aroma, and a pungent, bitter taste.

When roasted, the seeds lose their sharpness and develop a nutty aroma. Mixed with **coriander**, they also lose some of their bitter taste.

Cumin seeds are used whole or ground; their bitterness and pungent taste is more pronounced when

Saffron
As a powder or in the form of dried filaments, saffron is quite often used in the kitchen. One of the best kinds comes from Valencia, Spain. Saffron is used to season rice and Risotto, Paella, Bouillabaisse, seafood, tomato sauces and dishes, fish soups, scrambled eggs, white meat and grilled fish. Besides, it is used to spice Rouille and Picalilly, a spicy relish which is very popular in England. In Sweden, saffron is used in Christmas bread. Saffron gives a pretty yellow color to food.

used in powder form. **Cumin** is best kept in a sealed jar in a dark place.

Cumin also has medicinal properties: in India it is given against indigestion and stomach ache. It also has an effect against flatulence and colic; it stimulates the appetite and soothes the stomach; and it is a sudorific.

CURCUMA DOMESTICA   **Turmeric**
Family: Zingiberaceae
Origin: south India, Malaysia and Java
Height: 35.4 inches (90 cm)
Flowering: early summer
Properties: bactericide, laxative, digestive, stomachic

Turmeric is the fleshy root of a tropical aromatic plant belonging to the **ginger** family. **Turmeric** is used equally as a spice and a dye, which is why it is sometimes also called Indian **saffron**. It is a very ancient plant which has been grown for at least 2,000 years in India, China and in the Middle East. **Turmeric** is also mentioned as a coloring in old recipes from Assyrian times (600 BC).

Around 1450, it appeared, under the name of *temoe lawacq,* on a list of preparations which were sold in Frankfurt (Germany).

Turmeric is widespread in India where Hindus associate it with fertility and ascribe magic properties to it. Today, it is cultivated in all tropical regions of the world.

Turmeric is a perennial plant with abundant, elongated leaves and a projecting stem with yellow clustered flowers, resembling those of lilies or Calla. The root is a long, rhizome full of protuberances producing radicals on the lower layer and branches on the upper one. This rhizome has a peppery aroma and a pungent, somewhat bitter taste.

Turmeric is grown in fresh, deep soil in a sunny location. To breed a new plant, pieces of rhizome are planted 4 inches deep. Nine months later, they can be harvested.

Once they are dug out, the new rhizomes are cooked in order to peel off their skin. Then they are put in the sun to dry for a week.

Turmeric is mostly found as a yellowish-orange powder. However, in Asian grocery shops, the fresh root

is sometimes also available. **Turmeric** is used to alleviate liver diseases, to fight against bacteria, to promote bile activity, and to relieve ulcers.

Turmeric is also used in the manufacture of curry powder. It is also used as an adulterant of mustard and a substitute for it. Moreover it forms one of the ingredients of many cattle condiments. Tincture of **turmeric** is used as a coloring agent.

Cumin

In Germany, cumin seeds are mixed with flour to make bread, and are used in sauerkraut, pickles, sauces and cheese. In the Netherlands, Gouda cheese with cumin is a delicacy. Cumin flavors rice and dry legumes. In Mexico, it is an ingredient in Chili con Carne, and in Morocco it seasons soups and lamb. Because of its very spicy taste, it is used in small amounts. Cumin is frequently associated with Indian, Arab, Turkish and Mexican cuisines. It is an ingredient for curry mixtures and garam massala.

CURCUMA ZEDOARI **Shell ginger**

Family: Zingiberaceae
Origin: China and India
Height: 3.28 feet (1 m)
Flowering: summer
Properties: apéritif, bactericide, laxative, digestive, tonic, stimulant

Close to **turmeric**, **shell ginger** is an Asian spice which is often mistaken with the *Galanga kaempferia*. It came with the Arabs to Europe without becoming very successful. Today, it is used almost exclusively in the countries of origin.

This perennial plant has an aromatic, fleshy rhizome and very wide, big, radical leaves. Its yellow flowers are borne in dense long clusters on red and green

65

bracts. The flower petals form a shortened tube with three teeth and a large labellum (two or three fused stamens), giving an orchidlike appearance.

Its taste is bitter, but less sharp than that of **ginger**. Its smell is reminiscent of **camphor**. This herbaceous plant prospers in the nourishing ground of the tropical rain forests. It is bred by replanting pieces of rhizome that can be harvested after the second year, when they are then dried in the sun. The dried roots are available whole, minced or pulverized.

Shell ginger contains an essential oil and substances which stimulate the appetite and accelerate convalescence. Besides, it helps promote bile activity and is also considered an effective bactericide against infections.

Because it contains a highly nutritious and easy to digest starch, it can be given to people who are ill and small children.

Together with other spices like **turmeric** or **ginger**, **shell ginger** is used to prepare spicy pastes for seasoning white meat, poultry and fish. The powder also spices ragouts, stuffings, starchy food and sweets. With its natural pigment one can color silk.

DRIMYS LANCEOLATA, D. WINTERY   **Winter's bark**

Family: winteraceae
Origin: South America, Australia, South-East Asia, Madagascar
Height: 19.6 to 49.2 feet (6 to 15 m)
Flowering: spring to summer
Properties: antiscurvy, stimulant, stomachic, sudorific, tonic

---

Turmeric

Turmeric powder is applied to flavor canned food, rice, vegetables and numerous African and Asian dishes. It is also found in curry powder and is applied under the designation E 100 in order to dye spicy mustard, butter, some cheese sorts and liqueurs. Turmeric is also used in cosmetics and serves to dye textiles with a gentle yellow color. When using the fresh rhizomes, it is advisable to wear gloves because they stain the skin with a yellow color that will last for several days.

There are five genera of *Drimys*, which encompass altogether 60 species of trees and shrubs. For a long time, the plants have been associated with magnolias. However, they are closer to the *Cinnamomum* species, because of their aromatic bark, their evergreen leaves, and the regions where they grow.

The conical trees have a grey-brown, smooth bark which is very aromatic. Its smooth, margined leaves have an elongated, elliptic form, of about eight inches long and two inches wide. Their top side is dark green, and the bottom side is bluish. When ground, the leaves are very aromatic.

The white, flowers appear in big, bouquetlike clusters. The fruit, grouped on top of the stalk, are small green berries which turn brown to dark purple when ripe.

In medicine, the aromatic, bitter tasting bark which has vitamin C, an essential oil, tannin and alkaloids, is used.

The most sought out species is *Drimys wintery* from which the so called **winter's bark** is extracted. It was used in 1577, for the first time by **Captain William**

Winter, a companion of **Sir Francis Drake**, to cure his whole crew of scurvy. The sort *Drimys lanceolata* carries fruit which are used, after the drying and mincing process, like **pepper**.

The spice has a slight sourish, pungent taste that goes well with meat, sauces, vegetables and ragouts. There is *Drimys mexicana*, known as chachaca in Mexico, which is similar to *Drimys wintery*.

ELETTARIA CARDAMOMUM   **Cardamom**

Family: *Zingiberaceae*
Origin: *India, Sri Lanka*
Height: *several feet*
Flowering: *all year round*
Properties: *antiseptic, carminative, digestive, stomachic*

Cardamom, a herbaceous perennial shrub similar to a tall rose tree, has an underground rhizome. Even though it is cultivated, it grows wild in the forests of southern India. Its long, linear leaves reach up to 9.8 feet long. Its greenish-white flowers bloom all year round.

The fruit is a green, three sided capsule containing dark, reddish-brown to brownish-black, hard, angular, very fragrant seeds. The spice is made out of the ripe, dried fruit and the seeds.

It was only until the 19th century, that the plant was grown for the first time from seeds; however, the seedlings were sterile. Today, **cardamom** is cultivated in many tropical countries.

The plant is propagated by cutting the rhizome, but it takes three years for the first harvest which is carried out by hand. The main producing countries are India, Cambodia and Sri Lanka. This spice has been known in India for many years. The Egyptians sold and used it as a cure for bad breath. In Greece, it was used to make perfumes; in Rome, it was a digestive.

There are several species including: the **Malabar cardamom** (*Elettaria cardamomum minuscula* or *minor*), the smallest and most widely used, has an aroma similar to that of **lemon** and **eucalyptus**; and the **Ceylon cardamom** (*Elettaria cardamomum major*), also named **brown cardamom**, the biggest sort with an intense **camphor** aroma and grows wild in Sri Lanka.

Cardamom seeds contain cellulose, starch, proteins and essential oils which can be used in perfumery. They are also used in medicine against flatulence, stomach trouble and indigestion. Furthermore, they are a very good antiseptic.

Cardamom

There are cardamom capsules of different qualities: green cardamom, the most fragrant and widely used; white cardamom, which is bleached with chemicals losing its quality; and brown cardamom, with a distinct camphor taste. Cardamom is sold as powder, but it is heavier and loses its aroma rapidly. Cardamom is used in curry mixtures, and in gingerbread. In Indian cuisine it is very popular. In the Arab Emirates and in the Middle East, it is used to flavor tea and is considered to be a symbol of wealth. In Scandinavia, it is used in doughs and cake mixtures. In North Africa, is served with coffee and is used as a breath freshener. In Europe, cardamom is used in tea, ice cream, creams, cakes, compotes and fruit salads. It is used to season pickles, herring and aquavit.

EUCALYPTUS GLOBULUS   *Eucalyptus*
Family: *Myrtaceae*
Origin: *Tasmania*
Height: *114 feet (35 m plus)*
Flowering: *May to July*
Properties: *antiseptic, apéritif, astringent, bactericide, febrifuge, stimulant*

The **eucalyptus globulus** has a very spicy, balsamic essence that is used in its pure form only to make cigarettes and cough lozenges. Nevertheless, there is a tree of the same genus which, thanks to its minty aroma, can replace **eucalyptus** in the kitchen. This tropical tree grows in the Mediterranean basin.

It is mostly a large perennial tree which grows rapidly, attaining great height. Its ash-grey trunk is straight; it has a bark full of little openings which contain a balsamic gum.

Its wood is red. Young trees have opposite, light green, glossy leaves, whereas older trees have alternate,

stalked, rough, plain, pendent, sickle shaped ones. The white flowers have petals that cohere to form a cap that is shed when the flower blooms, releasing whorls of stamens grouped in bundles.

The fruit are hard, sharp edged, greenish blue capsules surrounded by a woody, cup shaped receptacle and numerous minute, dark seeds. The scent of **eucalyptus** is strong and very aromatic. The taste is aromatic as

well, but also bitter. The leaves are harvested in summer, dried and stored in a jar. **Eucalyptus** is rich in eugenol, tannin, and resins.

Eucalyptus is used to alleviate asthma and is recommended as an inhalant against colds, influenza and to alleviate sinusitis.

An **eucalyptus** compress alleviates and disinfects small wounds and insect bites. Its essential oil has a liquefying effect on secretions of the lungs, thus clearing them up. As a cough lozenge or syrup, **eucalyptus** works against coughs and soothes sore throats. Because of its bitterness, it is not often used in medical preparations. It is used in sweets and to make an apéritif.

In moderation, it can be used to enhance the flavor of ragouts and game. In the kitchen, peppery **eucalyptus** is preferred because of its minty taste. As a refreshing infusion, **eucalyptus** facilitates digestion and helps fight against bad breath.

In pharmaceutics, it is used in toothpastes, suppositories, injections and cooling gels. It is also used in skin care products.

The trees are planted in order to drain marshes, and their fragrance is used to keep insects away. The bark is used in tanning lotions; its wood, hard and highly resistant, is used in carpentry.

EUGENIA CARYOPHYLLATA — Clove

Family: Myrtaceae
Origin: probably the Moluccas
Height: 49 feet (15 m)
Flowering: summer
Properties: antiseptic, antispasmodic, sedative, healing agent, stimulant

---

Even though the Chinese have been using **clove**, the flower of the *Eugenia* also known as *Sysgium aromaticum* for centuries, it only appeared in Europe during the 8th century. This splendid tropical tree has always been coveted for the spice it produces. For a long time, the Portuguese had the monopoly of its cultivation because they owned the islands where the tree was grown.

At the beginning of the 18th century, Pierre Poivre succeeded in bringing the seeds out of the country. Afterwards, the plant was cultivated on the island of Mauritius by the Dutch and the French. Later, it made its way to the island of Zanzibar in Tanzania which is the world's largest producer of **clove**. It is also grown in Indonesia, Brazil and Madagascar.

Like any other **myrtle** plant, this evergreen tree has simple, opposite, gland-dotted and aromatic leaves. They are glossy green and can be up to 5 inches long. The flowers, arranged in terminal clusters at the end of young branches, have a funnellike calyx containing several stamens with yellow pistils, and a corolla of four pink petals. The dark purple fruit are elongated, tiny segmented berries.

Even though all the parts of the tree are aromatic, the buds which are handpicked and dried in the shade, are the ones used to obtain **clove**. In Zanzibar, harvesting, which takes place at least three times a year, is the main activity of the island.

Clove

Thanks to its pungent, sweet taste, whole or ground, clove flavors savory and sweet dishes alike. Onions studded with cloves are a traditional seasoning for broths and stews. It is also used in sauces, cooked ham, sauerkraut, pot roast, marinades and pickles. It is an ingredient in spice mixtures like Indian curry or Chinese five spice powder. It is used in the preparation of gingerbread, biscuits, and certain cakes. Its powder is used in apple pies and compotes. It spices mulled wine and bitter liqueurs. In Indonesia, it is used to perfume cigarettes or Kreteks.

Cloves, which have a particularly strong aroma, contain 21% of eugenol, an essential oil, tannin and resin.

Clove essence, obtained by distilling the buds and leaves of the plant, is used to soothe the stomach and as a local anaesthetic for toothache.

Clove is also used to alleviate intestinal problems, sore throats and in childbirth. Used in a compress, it helps heal wounds. It also facilitates sleep. In pharmaceutics, its antiseptic essence is used in toothpaste as it not only disinfects, but also refreshes breath.

In Tunisia, it is used to prepare *tidnissa*, a natural deodorant, with a delicate bitter scent, and *jbel boulah-nach*, the main component of henna.

In perfumery, **clove** is mixed with **ylang-ylang** to obtain high quality essences and potpourris. It is often used in sachets or pomanders, a **clove**-studded **orange**, **lemon** or apple, to perfume linen in closets.

EUGENIA UNIFLORA   **Surinam cherry**
Family: Myrtaceae
Origin: Brazil and the West Indies
Height: 16.4 to 23 feet (5 to 7 m)
Flowering: spring
Properties: stimulant, refreshing

The **Surinam cherry** is an evergreen tree or half shrub often planted as a hedge. Today, it grows in all tropical and subtropical regions, mainly in tropical America and in South-East Asia.

Its small oval, wine-red leaves take a shiny dark green color with age. Its creamy flowers, which appear separately or in clusters, produce a large, round, red fruit with a soft pulp and a spicy, sweet and sour taste.

Surinam cherries contain many vitamins and are consumed, raw or cooked, in sorbets, jellies and in beverages.

In South-East Asia, the green fruit are marinated in vinegar or **salt** to make a spice used to season meat and fish. They are also used to prepare chutney.

FERULA ASA FOETIDA   **Asafetida**
Family: Umbelliferae
Origin: Iran, Afghanistan, northern India
Height: 6.5 to 9.8 feet (2 to 3 m)
Flowering: summer
Properties: antispasmodic, emmenagogue, tonic

This gum resin is extracted from a tropical plant known as *Ferula foetida*. It has been used for many years in India and the Middle East. The Romans valued its distinct taste which is reminiscent of that of a mixture of onions and garlic.

This big perennial plant, with high grassy branches, has a fleshy root. Its flowers, which stand in umbels, develop small fruit. After four years, when the plant is ready to yield **asafetida**, the stems are cut down close to the root, and a milky juice flows out that quickly sets into a solid resinous mass with a consistency similar to that of wax. Due to the sulphurous essential oil it contains, the plant has a characteristic smell and taste which resembles that of garlic.

Asafetida can be found in different forms: as a resin, paste and powder. In medicine, it is used in pills or tinctures to soothe spasms, to relieve menstrual pain, and to treat nervous illnesses.

FOENICULUM VULGARE   **Fennel**
Family: Umbelliferae
Origin: southern Europe, Asia Minor
Height: 5 feet (1.5 m)
Flowering: June to August
Properties: antispasmodic, apéritif, sedative, diuretic, galactagogue, stimulant, stomachic, tonic

---

In antiquity, **fennel** was used to heal snake and scorpion bites. Pliny the Elder recommended it against blindness. There are all sorts of varieties of **fennel** with more or less sweet, peppery or bitter fruits.

With time, **fennel** spread west, and in the Middle Ages, its seeds were chewed in times of famine and during Lent to mitigate hunger. In those days, the plant was reputed to protect against evil, to preserve youth and vigor, and to guarantee good health.

This perennial plant has stalks with finely divided leaves composed of many linear or awl shaped segments, giving it a feathery look. The small yellow flowers, arranged in large terminal umbels, bear greenish-brown seeds with prominent longitudinal ridges. The stump of the tree, formed by the fleshy sheaths of the base, is strong and thick.

The whole plant has a very pleasant fragrance similar to that of **aniseed**.

Fennel, which can be used as a spice, an aromatic herb, and a vegetable, is easy to grow. It requires a light, well drained, relatively poor soil and a very sunny location. It is grown from seed or through the division of remaining clumps.

Generally, the parts of the plant that are used are the leaves, the fruit or seeds which are harvested after maturity in September and October, and the roots which are dug out after the first year.

In addition to an essential oil, **fennel** contains vitamins (A, B, and C) and mineral salts. Its roots have a positive effect on the urinary system; its seeds

---

Asafetida

Asafetida is very popular in the vegetarian dishes of Asian cuisine, where it is known as "delicacy of Gods." It is also used in curries and vinegar pickles. The pleasant smell of its powder and its root disappears with cooking. This spice goes well with vegetables and fish.

strengthen the stomach. Because it contains anethol, an essential oil, **fennel** is also prescribed for massages and infusions against flatulence. Its oil alleviates stomach cramps and colics. The oil can also be sprayed in the air to alleviate asthma and illnesses of the high respiratory tract.

The powdered seeds are used to keep fleas and other parasites away. When chewed, the seeds help fight against bad breath and stimulate digestion.

Besides, **fennel** promotes milk production. It is used in skin care products, hair rinses, soaps, and cough syrups. **Fennel** symbolizes flattery.

The tender leaves are often used for garnishes and to add flavor to salads; they are are also added to sauces.

GALACTODENDRON   *Cow tree, Milk tree* (BROSIMUM GALACTODENDRON)

Family: *Moraceae*
Origin: *South America*
Height: *82 to 98 feet (25 to 30 m)*
Flowering: *spring*
Properties: *astringent, digestive, nutritious, stimulant, tonic*

The **milk tree** is a tropical tree that does not produce a real spice, but from its juice an aromatic, tasty substance can be extracted. This useful tree, frequent in Venezuela and other countries of tropical and subtropical Americas, belongs to the same family of the Japanese silk mulberry tree and the fig tree.

This tree, which has probably existed since prehistoric times, is a tall evergreen. It has unmistakable, unisex flowers whose stamens project from the floral bud. Its fruit are dry.

The **milk tree** belongs to the latex producing plants. This easily recognizable, white substance is obtained by making an incision on the tree's bark.

The **milk tree** grows in dry, arid, rocky and mountainous regions. It can survive for several weeks without water and under the hot rays of the sun. Its leaves are leathery and dry, and its branches look as if they are dead.

However, upon cutting the bark of the trunk, a white liquid, which looks, tastes and has the same nutritional properties of milk, emerges. It has a balsamic smell and a very sweet taste. This milk produces an aro-

matic cream that, through evaporation, yields a paste similar to marzipan. Because it contains mineral salts, sugar, proteins and lipids, it is a very nutritional and digestive food.

The paste helps fight against anaemia, and promotes the growth of children. It is used in pastries, creams and puddings. It is curdled and mixed with stir-fried vegetables.

Fennel

Fennel is a popular spice used in grilling. It goes well with white meat and fatty fish like salmon, herring or mackerel. Its roasted seeds are added to ragouts and brines. As a powder it seasons salads and marinades. Coarsely crushed, it is used in doughs, sweet pastries and soups. Its delicate aniseed taste harmonizes with pork and lamb. Fennel is also known in the production of liqueurs like the Fenouillette and the Pastis which were already popular before the French revolution. Its pulverized seeds are an ingredient in curries and other spice mixtures. An infusion from its leaves is said to facilitate digestion.

The **breadfruit tree**, which is native of the Polynesian and Sunda islands, also belongs to this family of trees.

If the edible fruit are buried, after a period of time, a sort of fermented, digestive cheese is obtained. This peculiar cheese is exceptionally durable.

The wood of these trees is used to build boats; the phloem is used to make baskets.

GLEDITSIA TRIACANTHOS   **Honey locust**
Family: Leguminosae
Origin: North America
Height: 98 feet (30 m)
Flowering: summer
Properties: nutritious, stimulant, tonic

This thorny tree of the pea family, often found in gardens, is of slender growth and provides light, filtered shade. It grows in humid forests and on fertile soil. It bears long compound leaves divided into as many as thirty oval leaflets. Some leaves are doubly divided in which case the leaflets are more numerous and smaller.

The leaflets have a shining green color which becomes yellow in autumn. Small greenish white, bisexual flowers are borne in clusters in the leaf axils. The fruit is a flattened pod, up to about 18 inches long, sometimes sickle shaped and twisted. Brown beanlike seeds lie within, separated by a sticky, sweet tasting substance.

The reddish-brown wood is hard, strong and heavy. It resists humidity and decay, but it is not very pliable.

From the fermented pulp of the **honey locust** seeds, an alcoholic beverage is produced. The pulp is also dried and applied in the preparation of candies and sweet pastes.

Soy bean

Soy beans are used to produce a spicy sauce which is obtained by fermenting crushed, cooked soy beans, mixed with fermented rice – koji – and wheat. This sauce is one of the most often used seasonings in the world. According to the recipe and the kind of soy bean, the sauce varies in color, taste and intensity. There is black soy sauce, sold by itself or spiced; dark soy paste, used to prepare glazed duck; hoisin sauce; oyster sauce, and shoyu sauce among others. Red soy beans fermented in salty wine produce another delicious seasoning. This fragrant soy sauce is used to prepare exotic marinades for all sorts of meat and fish. It is also an ingredient for sweet and sour sauces used in Chinese dishes. Germinated soy bean seeds are an excellent vegetable. Tofu, which is rich in protein and used in vegetarian cuisine to substitute meat and cheese, is made with curd soya milk. Tempeh is a sort of compact purée made from cooked soy beans and flour. It is used with meat, sauces, grilled steak, and soups.

GLYCINE MAX	**Soy bean**

Family: *Leguminosae*
Origin: *China*
Height: *about 5 feet (1.5 m)*
Flowering: *late spring*
Properties: *mineralizing, strengthening, anti-cholesterol*

Soy beans, used as a spice, a vegetable and an oil with multiple purposes, have been grown in China and Japan for 5,000 years. They were introduced to Europe as a vegetable in the 18th century and were cultivated in Kew Gardens, near London. Despite the fact that **soy beans** were brought to France by missionaries coming from China in 1740, they were not cultivated in Europe until the 19th century. In 1804 they were introduced to the United States where they became quite successful.

In 1910, a cooperative for the production of **soy milk** was created in Paris. But it was not until after World War II that the high protein content of the **soy bean**, superior to that found in meat and vegetable oils, was discovered.

Today **soy beans** are grown in places like India, Korea, Africa, South America and, most of all, in the United States which is the principal producer and consumer of **soy bean** products.

The **soy bean** is an annual, erect, branching plant. Its root has numerous nodules containing bacteria known as rhizobium. The whole plant is covered with fine hairs with odd-pinnate, lobed leaves. Its white, self-fertilizing flowers appear in clusters on the axils of the leaf and bear fruit or pods which contain three to six

seeds. The **soy bean** may be cultivated in most types of soil, but it thrives in warm, subtropical climates in humid, well drained, sandy loam. It requires plenty of light and little care.

The whole plant can be used. The seeds are harvested not only to produce oil, but also to make soy sauce, soya milk and tofu. Besides, the germinated seeds can be consumed as a vegetable or used as livestock feed. The remaining plant components serve as a green fertilizer; the rhizobium in the roots enrich the ground with nitrogen.

Soy beans are rich in vitamin C and carbohydrates. The germs are low in calories. The seeds contain 35 to 40% of vegetable proteins, 20% of lipids and approximately 35% of carbohydrates, in addition to mineral salts and vitamins B and E.

Soy bean products have a mineralizing effect, and supply a lot of energy. The lecithin obtained from its seeds considerably reduces cholesterol levels and helps prevent arteriosclerosis. **Soy beans** contain high concentration of several compounds which have demonstrated anti-carcinogenic activity. These include isoflavonoids, protease inhibitors and phytic acid. The low incidence of breast and colon cancer in Japan and China has been partially attributed to the high consumption of soya.

Although rarely consumed, **soy bean** oil is used in the production of soaps, emulsions and colors. **Soy bean** flour is used in natural food.

In pharmaceutics, soy bean is used to produce milk and dietary products. It is an important nutritional and industrial plant.

GLYCYRRHIZA GLABRA	**Licorice**

Family: *Papilionaceae*
Origin: *Mediterranean region*
Height: *3.2 feet (1 m)*
Flowering: *June to July*
Properties: *antispasmodic, expectorant, emollient, stomachic*

Licorice is a very ancient plant known for its medicinal properties in Egypt and China. The name **licorice**, which describes its sweet, slightly bitter flavor, comes from the greek word *glykyrrhiza* or "sweet root."

The Arabs cultivated the plant for the first time in Spain during the 9th century from where it spread on to Italy and later to Central Europe, Russia and Turkey. Today, the main producing countries are Turkey, the Middle Eastern countries, Spain, the south-Italian province of Calabria, and the south of France.

Licorice is a perennial herb with robust, projecting branches. It has pinnate leaves with green, oval leaflets which have a viscous underside. In the summer, axillary clusters of blue or lilac, oblong flowers appear. Its fruit are flattened pods which contain three to four brown seeds. Its root is segmented and formed by a rhizome which can reach up to 3.2 feet in length. It is soft, fibrous, and flexible with a sweet, sugary taste. When they are four years old, the roots are gathered and used. They are put to dry and shredded or cut into sticks. The dried root sticks are brown and wrinkled due to

dehydration and their inner part is yellow because it contains several flavone pigments.

Licorice contains carbohydrates, tannin, flavonoid, lots of saponine, as well as glycyrrhizin whose structure is similar to that of cortisone, and phytoestrogens. In 1950, it was discovered that flavone pigments protect the stomach against ulcers and can contribute to their healing.

Licorice
To produce a refreshing beverage, licorice is dissolved in water. Its pulverized root is used in beverages, pastries, fruit salads and sorbets. Licorice also perfumes chewing gum, candy, syrups, and different liqueurs like Pastis and Raki.

Licorice is not only recommended for people who suffer from stomach disorders, it is also used to fight high blood pressure. Because it contains glycyrrhizin, also known as "vegetable cortisone," it works with the minerals of the body lowering blood pressure. In small amounts, it is recommended as a cough suppressant, to soothe hoarseness, and to alleviate stomach cramps. The main ingredient glycyrrhizin has also been studied for its anti-viral properties in the treatment of AIDS. In clinical trials in Japan it prevented progression of the HIV virus by inhibiting cell infection and inducing interferon activity. **Licorice** candy can be chewed for pleasure or as breath refresher.

There is a variety of this plant, *Glycyrrhiza echinata*, to be found in Italy, which was most probably the one used in antiquity.

ILLICIUM VERUM　　　　　**Star aniseed**

Family: *Magnoliaceae*
Origin: *China, Japan, warm regions of America*
Height: *19.6 to 26 feet (6 to 8 m)*
Flowering: *spring*
Properties: *antiseptic, antispasmodic, apéritif, carminative, digestive, eupeptic, stomachic*

The **star aniseed** is the fruit of a shrub with white bark and evergreen leaves. The shrub only produces fruit after the sixth year; however, it lives up to one hundred years.

Its leaves are elongated, smooth and glossy. Its large yellowish flowers stand separately on the leaf axils. They are quite decorative and, like the whole shrub, quite fragrant.

At maturity the flower produces a characteristic star shaped fruit composed of a ring and several joined podlike follicles, each of which opens along one seam to release a single light brown, smooth, lustrous seed.

The fruit are harvested before they are ripe, while they are still green, and placed to dry in the sun where they become hard and turn reddish-brown.

Whole **star aniseed** can be kept for a long time in an airtight container in a dark place. As a powder it loses relatively quickly its aroma. The fragrance of this spice resembles that of **aniseed** which has a more pungent, sweeter taste.

The Chinese believe that **star aniseed** leaves, which they have used for centuries, have stomach-strengthening properties. They give aroma to their tea with **star aniseed**, which they believe is an antidote to many poisons, and burn it to perfume the air. **Star aniseed** was introduced to Europe in the 17th century.

Since it was brought from Russia, where it was considered a magical plant, it was first known as **Siberian aniseed**. Siberians believed that the smoke of the burned seeds increased psychic powers.

In France, it was used to flavor alcoholic drinks such as Ratafia and Anisette. Today, its essential oil, anethole, is used to facilitate digestion and fight loss of appetite.

In pharmaceutics, anethole is applied to the production of cough syrups. It is also used in soaps, perfumes, sweets and alcoholic beverages.

Furthermore, **star aniseed** wood is used in inlaid wood work.

Star aniseed

Star aniseed is used often in Chinese and Vietnamese dishes to season poultry, pork and beef stews. It is an important component of the Chinese five spice powder. It is also used against bad breath.

JUNIPERUS COMMUNIS　　　　**Juniper**

Family: *Cupressaceae*
Origin: *Europe, the Middle East*
Height: *19.6 feet (6 m)*
Flowering: *April to June*
Properties: *anti-rheumatic, antiseptic, aperitif, diuretic, sudorific*

Juniper is for the first time mentioned in the Old Testament: as a boy, Jesus hid behind its foliage from the Roman soldiers who were pursuing him. Afterwards, the tree was consecrated to the virgin Mary.

In Italy it is considered a protecting tree; in the Middle Ages its twigs were hung above the front door to keep evil out. Today, **juniper** is cultivated because of its aromatic berries, its medicinal properties, and its wood.

The most important countries where **juniper** is grown are Hungary and Southern European countries such as Italy, which produces particularly aromatic berries.

Juniper is a small, evergreen, sprawling shrub. Its trunk has a reddish or grey bark with branches that carry bluish-green, needlelike leaves arranged in pairs or whorls of three. Male and female reproductive structures usually are borne on separate plants: male plants have a conical shape while female ones are spread out. The latter carry the flowers which stand on the leaf axils and are hardly visible. The fruit are dark blue berries which, upon maturity, have a greyish, waxy covering.

During the first year, the berries are green, maturing only the next autumn. That is why, on the same female plant, there are at the same time green and ripe fruit.

The ripe fruit are harvested with gloves because the branches have very sharp thorns. After the harvest they are set in the shade to dry slowly.

Juniper thrives on hard, well permeable, stony ground and sunny locations. It is grown from seed or by grafting.

This small conifer contains tannin, flavonoid and organic acids. Its berries have a bitter sweet taste and a fragrance resembling that of turpentine.

Juniper has a history of medicinal usage dating as far as 1550 BC. A remedy to treat tapeworm was found in an ancient Egypt papyrus. It is taken in infusions to ease digestion, but in high dosage it can irritate the urinary tract. In ointments, it is used against aching muscles. Its essential oil mixed with sweet almond oil produces a relaxing massage balm.

Juniper is also used in order to scent bath essences and soaps, as well as other skin care products, and in perfumes. It is known that the branches and berries were burned in ancient Egypt temples as a part of purification ceremonies.

In many European dishes, especially in the Alpine regions, where **juniper** grows abundantly, it is an important spice.

From the berries a bluish color is obtained which serves – mixed with alum – as a yellow coloring agent.

Furthermore, its wood is extremely popular in the making of cigar boxes. It is still used today in carpentry and inlaid wood work. **Juniper** symbolizes protection.

Juniper

In former times, juniper berries were used as a substitute for pepper. In the 18th century, a juniper wine, known as "wine of the poor," was produced by fermenting water, juniper, and absinthe. Juniper berries are used whole for marinades, broths, braised dishes, ragouts and sauerkraut. Ground, it flavors stews, rabbit, and game. In cakes, fruit pies or apple compote, it is delicious. The most famous alcoholic drinks made with juniper berries are gin, aquavit and some Swedish beers. Its branches and roots are used in smoked ham, salmon and some sausages.

MANGIFERA INDICA — Mango

Family: *Anacardiaceae*
Origin: *North-East India, Burma*
Height: *98 feet (30 m)*
Flowering: *after the rainy season*
Properties: *antiscurvy, purifier, mineralizing*

Mango is a noble fruit which is highly valued in India. The **mango** tree has been cultivated there for more than 3500 years, and it is to this day an essential nutritional fruit. It arrived in Africa most probably during the 10th century with the Moors. In the 16th century and thanks to the Portuguese, it made its way into South America, foremost in Brazil. Since then, it is also grown in the Antilles and the Middle East, but Asia continues to

be its principal producer. The **mango** tree is a rounded, wide spread, evergreen with a thick, dark green foliage. Its alternating, leaves are lanceolate and up to 12 inches long. When they are young they have a red color that turns green as they age.

It has numerous yellowish-green flowers which are borne in large terminal panicles. The fruit varies greatly in size and character; the smallest **mangoes** are no larger than plums, while others may weigh four to five pounds.

The **mango** is an elongated, oval fruit with a thick, smooth skin of waxy appearance. Some varieties are vividly colored with shades of red and yellow, while others are dull green. The single flat seed is surrounded by a yellow to orange flesh, juicy and of distinctive spicy taste.

There is, however, another variety of **mango** whose pulp remains green when ripe. **Mangoes** thrive in all subtropical climate zones, and propagation is done by grafting or budding.

Mango contains a lot of sugar and is a good source of energy and nutrition. It is rich in vitamins A, B and C, as well as mineral salts.

MONODORA MYRISTICA   *Jamaica or Calabash nutmeg*

Family: *Anonaceae*
Origin: *West Africa*
Height: *65.6 feet (20 m)*
Flowering: *spring*
Properties: *astringent, purifier, diuretic, febrifuge, narcotic, sedative*

Also known as calabash, the **Jamaica nutmeg** is a tree that arrived with the slave trade in India and tropical South America. Originally it was used as an ornamental plant, but it began to be used as a spice due to its distinct **nutmeg** aroma.

In the wild, the tree reaches a considerable height, but when cultivated it is kept relatively small. Its large leaves of approximately 16 inches long are alternate, oblong, rough, red when young and later green.

Its pendulous flowers appear in long stalks and are arranged on the leaf axils. They are dicot, yellow and spotted with a reddish-brown color. They consist of a chalice with six sepals and a corolla of three petals with waved edges and numerous stamens. The single carpel contains one basal ovule.

The flowers bear fleshy fruit reminiscent of big, oval berries. They have a hard, woody rind and a pulp with numerous seeds whose taste is similar to that of **nutmeg**.

Once the seeds are harvested, they are dried in the sun to produce a spice which is valued not only because of its sweet, pungent taste, but also because of its medicinal properties.

The seeds contain myristicin, an essential oil, as well as carbohydrates, mineral salts, and small quantities of vitamins A and C. In small amounts, it facilitates digestion, alleviates flatulence and rheumatic pain, and works as an expectorant.

Its seeds are used to spice vegetables, meat, fish, sauces, stuffings, gratins and starchy food. They give fruit salads and apéritifs an interesting, peppery, sweet note. Its aroma is also used in perfumes and skin care products.

In the same family, there are other trees with particular qualities, like the *Anona ethiopica* which is used to produce a peppery spice used in Ethiopian cuisine and in medicine; the *Cananga odorata*, also known as a **ylang-ylang**, used in the perfume industry; and the *Asimina triloba* used in the United States to produce fermented, aromatic, sour beverages.

The wood of **Jamaica nutmeg** is popular in carpentry and used in inlaid wood work because it is not too hard, but compact, heavy and of excellent quality.

MONSTERA DELICIOSA   *Philodendron or Ceriman*

Family: *Araceae*
Origin: *Central and South America*
Height: *about 32 feet (10 m)*
Flowering: *spring*
Properties: *anti-inflammatory, apéritif, diuretic, tonic*

The *Monstera* is one of the most important varieties of the **philodendron** species that is usually found in the tropics.

It is a very popular climbing plant with strong branches. The young leaves are entire, green and shaped like a heart. When they grow, they become variously lobed and cut with small perforations on each side of the central vein.

The leaves have stalks that can be up to 7.8 inches long, with old ones reaching up to 27 inches and up to 15.7 inches wide. Its inflorescence is a leaflike cone or spathe, green to white or reddish, which surrounds a central stout spadix bearing hermaphrodite flowers. Wrapped in a rough whitish envelope, the spathe, which is at first closed, opens slowly until blooming.

Its fruit, known as **ceriman**, which are yellow at first and becoming purple with maturity, are formed by a cylindrical ovary covered by numerous berries. They are sweet, juicy and have a pleasant scent. Their flavor is similar to that of a mixture of banana and pineapple.

Mango

Mango is consumed fresh as a whole fruit, in fruit salads or as a fruit juice. It is used as an ingredient for jams and chutneys. The green variety is considered a vegetable which lends aroma to different sauces. Cooked green mangoes are cut, dried in the sun, and then ground to a powder which is then mixed with a pinch of turmeric. The sour spice thus obtained is known in India as "amchoor", (from "am" which means mango and "choor" for powder) and is used as a substitute for lemon or tamarind to season vegetable dishes. It is also suitable for ragouts, rice, soups, stuffings, marinades, meat and fish, as well as some pastries, curries and chutneys. Mango, along with banana, is one of the most important fruits in the Indian diet.

The **ceriman** fruit consists of sugar, water, a proteolysis enzyme, mineral salts, **lime** oxalate, and vitamins A, B, and C. It is used to alleviate edema and pain in the joints. It helps clean the organism, and because of the vitamins it contains, it is a very nutritious fruit.

Because of its delicate taste resembling that of pineapple, **ceriman** juice is used to produce refreshing beverages and delicious ice cream desserts. It is used to spice sparkling wines and fruit juices, as well as roast pork. Its characteristic aroma can be used to make pancakes. The fruit itself can be flamed with rum or roasted. Furthermore, **philodendrons** are attractive house plants which require a humid, nutritious soil, but little light.

MORINGA OLEIFERA   **Horseradish tree**
Family: Moringaceae
Origin: North-East Africa and India
Height: 32.8 feet (10 m)
Flowering: after the rainy season
Properties: antiscurvy, digestive, diuretic, emollient, stimulant

---

The **horseradish tree** has been cultivated for many years as a useful, ornamental plant. Earlier it was classified as Capparidaceae, but today, it belongs to the *Moringaceae,* a family consisting of only one genus and a dozen species which have adapted themselves to dry conditions.

The horseradish tree has a thick, smooth trunk with few branches. Its leaves are bipinnate, oblong and soft green. Its cream colored flowers of five petals appear in big, hanging clusters, and because they contain a lot of nectar, they attract numerous birds. Its thin, brown fruit look like hanging, triangular pods and contain three rows of winged seeds.

The parts of the tree which are used are its leaves, its ripe seeds and its root. The whole plant has a pungent taste because it contains sulphur compounds which are bitter and stimulating, similar to those found in some *Cruciferae.*

The tree also contains alkaloids, mineral salts, tannin, slime, carbohydrates and vitamin C. As a medicinal plant, it is used to facilitate digestion and in hair treatment products. The juice from the roots is used in compresses against inflammations and swellings, and is taken against angina. Because it is rich in vitamin C, the plant is used against scurvy and to prevent colds. The oil

from the seeds is applied to heal skin irritations. Its juice also helps clean the body of impurities.

The bark produces a latex which is easily dissolved in water and is used as a finish for binding cotton textiles. Its oil is used to produce soaps, hair care products, and body creams. Besides, it is used to produce ben oil which is used as a lubricant for watches.

MURRAYA KOENIGII   *Orange jasmine*
Family: Rutaceae
Origin: South India and Sri Lanka
Height: 6.5 to 9.8 feet (2 to 3 m)
Flowering: spring
Properties: purifier, emollient, refreshing, stimulant

This tropical half shrub is named after **J. A. Murray** who back in the 18th century published the *Linnaeus Systema Vegetabilum*. It is formed by rough, bipinnate leaves with alternate leaflets which are dark green on the top side and pale green on the bottom.

Its leaflets, which are widely used in Indian cuisine to prepare curries, have a particularly pungent fragrance when ground.

Fresh or dried, they are used to give the simplest food a characteristic curry aroma. They are used in Indian dishes like opuma, or salted semolina, dried haricot beans and soups. It gives aroma to curries, marinades and omelettes; it is an ingredient in the madras curry mixture and shellfish sauces.

Orange jasmine infusions are used to lower blood pressure; ground and mixed with rice flour it alleviates intestinal problems.

Orange jasmine is easily found in Asian grocery shops. It can be kept fresh in the refrigerator or in the freezer. Vacuum packed, it keeps its aroma and color for long periods of time.

MYRICA GALE, M. RUBRA   *Sweet gale or Bog myrtle*

Family: Myriaceae
Origin: Europe, North America
Height: 3.28 feet (1 m)
Flowering: spring
Properties: antidiarrhoea, astringent, antiseptic, insecticide

---

Horseradish tree

Its root is used like horseradish. It is grated to season sauces. It is added into salad, stuffings, and soups. It is processed into a paste which is served as a relish with meat and fish. The leaves and the young fruits, which taste like cress, are prepared like any other vegetable. They also serve in order to lend aroma to herbal stuffings and sauces, in salads, and with curries. Its light, odorless oil does not become rancid. It is excellent for salad dressings.

The **sweet gale** shrub grows on damp and swampy ground in temperate regions. Its bark is reddish-brown with white spots. It has alternate, elongated, grey-green leaves with serrated edges and short stalks.

Shortly before the foliage blooms, red-brown catkins appear. These in turn, bear waxy, orange cherries. The whole plant gives off an intensely resinous scent.

Sweet gale is a sort of plant whose gender can vary from year to year: depending on the year, flowers are separately male and female on the same or different plants.

This plant is grown from the seed, by grafting or budding in humid, acid soil and in the shade. In winter the shrub must be cut back so that it has plenty of sprouts in the spring.

The leaves, the berries, the root and the bark are normally used. The leaves and berries can be dried without them losing their properties.

Because **sweet gale** contains an essential oil, tannin, yellow pigments, vitamin C, maleic acid, and citric acid, this plant has different medical properties. In an infusion it works against dysentery; in a compress it disinfects wounds and pimples. The essential oil is used to massage sprains and pulled muscles. Inhaled it alleviates colds, bronchitis and cough.

Its leaves and berries have a spicy, resinous taste which can be used not only to season game, grilled pork and ragouts, but also certain pastries. The berries can be added to fruit salads, and the leaves can be used to prepare deliciously, fragrant herbal teas.

Its dried leaves and its essential oil are used to perfume the linen in a closet and to keep insects away, especially to keep fleas away from rugs and pet baskets. A yellow coloring, used to dye cotton, wool and leather, is obtained from the bark and the roots of this shrub.

There is a related oriental variety of this plant – *Myrica rubra* – which is grown as an herb because its seeds are used as a spice.

MYRISTICA FRAGRANS **Nutmeg and Mace**
Family: *Myristacea*
Origin: *the Moluccas, Banda (Indonesia)*
Height: *32.8 feet (10 m)*
Flowering: *all year round*
Properties: *carminative, narcotic*

Nutmeg

Mace and nutmeg have an intense, spicy aroma. Their very aromatic and sweet flavor is used equally to season both savory and sweet dishes. Either can be ground or grated, always shortly before serving to ensure that they retain their aroma. They are used to prepare béchamel sauce, omelettes, vegetables, meat, mashed potatoes, pastes, soufflés, quiches, potato pies and soups. They also go well with fruit salads, Mousse au Chocolat, fruit flans, fruit pies, biscuits and other pastries, liqueurs, and mulled wines.

In the Middle Ages this tree was strongly coveted because **nutmeg** was one of the most expensive commercial spices.

In 1512, the Portuguese seized the group of islands of the Moluccas gaining control over the exploitation of this spice until the arrival of the Dutch, who controlled it until 1864 when its cultivation became free. The Dutch tried all kinds of ploys to keep the prices of **nutmeg** and **mace** high. They even burned down their own spice warehouses in Amsterdam. It is also said that, before being sold, they would dip the whole **nutmegs** in **lime** to prevent their sprouting.

In spite of all these precautionary measures, birds carried the seeds on to neighboring islands. In this way, **Pierre Poivre**, a Frenchman, succeeded – without particular secrecy and under the nose of the Dutch – to plant the seeds on the islands of Mauritius and Réunion where he had been appointed administrator from 1767 to 1773. In this way, **nutmeg** cultivation expanded and the spice became available worldwide.

Today **nutmeg** is grown in Sri Lanka, India, South-East Asia, Malaysia, Jamaica and the Caribbean islands.

This evergreen tree has a pyramid-shaped growth and rough, intensely aromatic, scented leaves of elongated, oval shape with a dark green top side and a whitish underside. The white flowers, arranged separately or in groups of three on the leaf axils, resemble those of the lily of the valley.

The **nutmeg** fruit is a pendulous, orange drupe, similar in appearance to an apricot. When fully mature it splits in two, exposing a crimson colored, fibrous, aril, the **mace**, surrounding a single shiny, brown seed, the **nutmeg**.

Nutmegs are dried gradually in the sun over a period of six to eight weeks. During this time, the **nutmeg** shrinks away from its hard seed coat until the kernels rattle in their shell when shaken. The shell is then broken and the **nutmeg**s are picked out. The **mace** is also dried and in the process it aquires its orange color.

Mace has a sweet, slightly warm taste similar to that of **nutmeg**, but finer. Because the **nutmeg** tree grows slowly, it is dioecious, and bears fruit only after 15 to 20 years, its culture is rather luxurious. Male and female trees must be planted together sheltered from the sun and the wind. They need a warm climate with damp, well permeable earth which contains plenty of nourishing humus. Only the adult female trees bear fruits.

Harvesting is done after the 15th year, three times a year and for approximately 40 to 60 years. A single **nutmeg** tree produces about 1,500 to 2,000 fruit in the course of its life. **Nutmeg** contains equal amounts of oil and starch, an essential oil, and myristicin, a toxic and euphoriant narcotic which in large amounts can be deadly.

In former times nutmeg was believed to have a number of different properties: it was considered to be an aphrodisiac which in addition alleviated rheumatism, difficulty in breathing and flatulence.

Today, due to its toxicity, **nutmeg** is hardly ever used in medicine. However, as a pleasantly, fragrant spice, it is still popular in the kitchen.

The essential oils extracted from **mace** are used to produce some perfumes and related products like soaps and shampoos.

MYRTUS COMMUNIS — *Myrtle*

Family: *Myrtaceae*
Origin: *Mediterranean region*
Height: *9.8 to 19.6 feet (3 to 6 m)*
Flowering: *May to July*
Properties: *antidiarrhoea, antiseptic, astringent, balsamic, emollient*

The evergreen foliage of this shrub and its fragrance have been a source of inspiration for poets. The Greeks consecrated the **myrtle** tree to Venus, and one of the three Graces carried a **myrtle** bouquet. Statues of great men were decorated with **myrtle**, and the Romans used it as an emblem for conjugal unity.

In the Old Testament, the young women of Israel carried **myrtle** wreaths on their wedding day. Its wood was burned as incense, and its medicinal properties have been acknowledged since antiquity.

Today, **myrtle** is cultivated mainly as an ornamental shrub in gardens. This shrub has a red-brown, flaky bark. Its rough, opposite, dark green leaves are thick, oval, pointed, and lustruous, with many small, translucent, oil bearing glands.

The solitary white flowers, which have a peppery aromatic fragrance, are borne on short stalks. The fruit, which mature in autumn, are oval, purplish-black berries with the size of a pea, and have a sharp resinous taste.

Myrtle

Myrtle leaves are used to season lamb, beef, poultry and fatty fish like herring and mackerel. Its fruit can be added to fruit salads and red fruit pies. In Corsica a delicious liqueur, the Myrtéi, is produced from its juice. Its dried flower buds are also used as a spice. They have a peppery taste which goes well with stuffings, sausages, different sauces and vegetables. Adding a pinch of myrtle powder to red currant or plum marmalade gives them an original, peculiar flavor.

The whole plant can be used: the fresh or dried leaves, the buds, the flowers, the fresh or dried fruits, the roots and the bark. **Myrtle** grows in temperate climates in fertile, permeable, preferably acid soil.

Myrtle contains essential oil, tannin, maleic acid, citric acid and vitamin C; therefore, it has several medicinal properties. The ground leaves disinfect and help heal small wounds, rashes and skin irritation. They are also used against dysentery.

The juice of the berries alleviates stomach problems, indigestion and haemorrhoids. The essential oil is very effective against colds, cough and bronchitis.

In perfumery, its leaves and flowers are distilled to obtain an extract known as "angel's water" which is used in soaps, shampoos and other body care products. Its essential oil is also used to make perfumes. The bark and roots are used in the tanning of leather. In the ornamental garden, **myrtle** is often preferred because its tight foliage can be easily shaped. In the south of France and Italy, hedges are frequently **myrtle** shrubs. Burnt **myrtle** wood has a very pleasant scent.

NIGELLA SATIVA — **Black cumin or Fennel flower**

Family: *Ranunculaceae*
Origin: *West Asia and Mediterranean region*
Height: *23.6 inches (60 cm)*
Flowering: *summer*
Properties: *apéritif, stimulant*

Also known as **allspice**, **black cumin** is in no way related to its namesake. It does not belong to the same family nor does it have the same geographic origin.

Black cumin is a small plant which is to be found frequently in wheat fields. Today it is cultivated mainly in India where its spicy seeds are very popular.

It is an annual herbaceous plant which the Romans named Nigellus, meaning "darkish." Its greyish-green leaves are divided in many lobes giving the plant a featherlike appearance. Its solitary blue flowers of five petals appear at the top of the branches. Its small, round fruit are partitioned in five segments containing numerous black seeds. These seeds are harvested and used as a peppery spice with a delicate **lemon** scent. **Black cumin** is sown in the spring and blooms in summer.

Black cumin needs average, permeable soil and a sunny location. The seeds, which contain lipids, essential oils, mineral salts, and vitamins, stimulate the production of digestive secretions and work against indigestion.

There is a close relative of this plant known as love-in-a-mist (*Nigella damascena*) which is predominantly used as an ornamental plant in gardens. This variety which is quite striking due to its featherlike appearance, stands out because of its celestial blue flowers and its very decorative fruit which once dried are often used in bouquets.

Its seeds are also used as a spice, but they are less fragrant and tasty.

PANDANUS TECTORIUS   **Screw pine**

Family: Pandaneae
Origin: India and China
Height: 16.4 feet (5 m)
Flowering: summer
Properties: antidiarrhoea, abortive

This sort of palm tree is widely spread throughout India and China.

The **screw pine** has a simple trunk covered with ringlike stigma left behind by dead leaves. It produces from its trunk and branches stiltlike aerial prop roots that support the plants and give them a distinctive appearance. The numerous, narrow, parallel veined, palmlike leaves with spiny margins are produced in tufts at the branch tips in close twisted ranks around the stem, forming screwlike helices of leaves. Its fragrant flowers are simple, petalless, usually densely clustered, and either male or female, with sexes produced in different plants.

The male flowers form branched out ears and are fitted with numerous stamens. The female flowers possess several rugged, monospermous ovaries. Its fruits are heavy ball shaped or conelike fibrous aggregates containing a single seed.

The **screw pine** contains essential oil, tannin, sugar, mineral salts, and vitamins. Its ripe fruit are used against dysentery, but when immature they can cause miscarriages. The fruit can be enjoyed fresh, in a salad or fruit pie. They are also used to make syrups, compotes and jam. A pleasantly fragrant spice is obtained from its flowers, which is not only used to season meat and vegetables, but also as an ingredient in cakes, sweets and beverages. Because of its intense fragrance, the plant is used in the production of perfumes, soaps and hair care products. It is also used in the cosmetics industry and to scent tobacco.

The **screw pine** is not only a useful nutritious plant, it can also be used as an ornamental tree like the palm tree.

Black cumin

It is advisable to roast the seeds of black cumin before consumption so that they release their full aroma. Black cumin is contained in different mixed spices like the Bengali five spice powder. It is frequently used in Indian cuisine in pickles and chutneys. Pulverized it seasons salads, vegetable ragouts, ratatouille, potatoes, compotes, and jams. Its aroma is also used in marinated and grilled fish, meat and poultry. In India, the seeds are mixed into breads like naan. In the Middle East it is used in breads and cakes with or without sesame seeds.

PAPAVER SOMNIFERUM   **Opium poppy**

Family: *Papaveraceae*
Origin: *Greece, Egypt, Asia Minor*
Height: *3.28 feet (1 m)*
Flowering: *late spring to early summer*
Properties: *tranquilizer, antispasmodic, expectorant, refreshing, sedative*

Of the numerous other members of this family, **opium poppy** is the most famous.

The plant is an annual evergreen. In ancient times Arab traders brought it to India, Persia and South-East Asia. The Greeks already knew of the anaesthetizing effects of opium and used it in medicine. The Romans dried the seeds and mixed them with honey to produce sweets.

Today **opium poppy** is cultivated in a many countries. On the one hand it is used as a spice, and on the other hand, it is used as an oil, pretty much like sunflower oil. Because its culture and commercialization is forbidden, the seeds of the *Papaver rhoeas* variety, which have no negative side effects, are the ones exploited for culinary use.

Opium poppy is an annual, herbaceous plant with smooth, spread out branches which carry lobed or unevenly dissected or serrated leaves. It has large, terminal flowers. They are red, or bluish-pink with black spots at the base of their petals and numerous stamens surrounding the ovary. The ovary develops in the form of an ovoid capsule which is partitioned inside into 4 to 14 segments containing numerous dark purple or yellow seeds, according to the species. Once the capsules are ripe, they are harvested for their seeds which have an almondlike taste.

Because the unripe capsules contain a milky sap, composed of two alkaloids – morphine and narcotine – the **poppy** plant has a sedative effect on the nervous system. Besides it contains codeine which is used to suppress coughs, and papaverine which is used as an antispasmodic. Because of these active substances, **opium poppy** has a variety of pharmaceutical applications.

The seeds of the **opium poppy** contain a substance rich in phosphorus – lecithin – starch, oil, sugar, mineral salts, and vitamins. Thanks to their lecithin content, the seeds help control and lower cholesterol levels.

Poppy oil is not only used in the production of soaps, creams and lotions, but also in the manufacture of paint and lacquers.

Poppy

Poppy seeds have a taste similar to that of nuts or almonds. They are used whole, dry or ground. They are added to salads, sauces, milk puddings, cakes and fruit salads. They are used in breads and pastries. Ground poppy is added to curries to make them thick and enhance their flavor. Roasted, they are used in tomato salads, sauerkraut and with potatoes. Germinated poppy seeds are eaten as a vegetable or as an ingredient for salads. Poppy oil is extracted from the seeds and is used for light, tasty vinaigrettes.

PEUMUS BOLDUS   **Boldo**

Family: *Monimiaceae*
Origin: *South America*
Height: *19.6 feet (6 m)*
Flowering: *summer*
Properties: *laxative, stomachic, stimulant*

The **boldo** is a fragrantly scented shrub which is to be found wild on the sunny slopes of Chile. The native Indians have always used its leaves as a spice and for their medicinal properties.

The shrub has small, elliptic, rough, dark green leaves which give off a scent similar to that of mint. They contain **eucalyptus** oil, alkaloids like boldine, and flavonoid.

The shrub has small, elliptic, rough, dark green leaves which give off a scent similar to that of mint. They contain **eucalyptus** oil, alkaloids like boldine, and flavonoid.

Boldo is a plant that strengthens the stomach and stimulates the appetite. Besides, it promotes gall bladder activity and is contained in different medicaments which are prescribed against liver diseases.

Because of its mintlike aroma, it can be used, in small amounts, as a spice and to facilitate digestion.

PHYLLANTHUS ACIDUS   **Otaheite gooseberry**

Family: *Euphorbiaceae*
Origin: *South-East Asia*
Height: *32.8 feet (10 m)*
Flowering: *all year round*
Properties: *purifier, purgative, revitalizer, stimulant, tonic*

By the end of 18th century, the **otaheite gooseberry** was imported to the Antilles and to America.

The **otaheite gooseberry** is a small tree which is cultivated in tropical regions because of its acid-sour fruit. The tree carries a few, relatively tight, upright branches. It has long deciduous twigs lined with rows of sharply pointed, alternating, light green leaves, two to three inches (6 to 7 cm) long. Its inconspicuous, red flowers, which have six petals, are grouped in dangling clusters. The **otaheite gooseberry** flowers bear fruit during the whole year. The yellowish-green fruits are small, flat, rounded drupes divided internally into several chambers containing in each case two seeds.

The **otaheite gooseberry** is a sour-spicy, very refreshing fruit. Because it is rich in pectins, carbohydrates, mineral salts, and vitamin C, it facilitates digestion. Moreover, it is used during convalescence, and helps alleviate colds and influenza and invigorates the whole body. Thanks to the pectins it contains, it slows the appetite and reduces calorie intake: this is why it is used in weight-loss diets. Its very acid fruit can be eaten raw, with sugar or as a seasoning. It can be used to make jams and fruit preserves. The juice is used to lend aroma to different beverages. Its sour taste also goes well with fish and light broths.

PIMENTA DIOÏCA	Allspice

Family: *Myrtaceae*
Origin: *the Antilles, South America*
Height: *32.8 to 39.3 feet (10 to 12 m)*
Flowering: *spring*
Properties: *antiseptic, aromatic, carminative, digestive*

Allspice, also known as **pimento** or **Jamaica pepper**, owes its name to the fact that the flavor of its dried berries resembles a combination of **pepper**, **clove**, **cinnamon** and **nutmeg**. The spice was introduced to Europe by **Christopher Columbus** who mistakenly took it to be a type of **pepper**.

The **allspice** tree is erect with a thin, pale green bark which peels away annually. This evergreen has splendid, oblong, rough leaves. The white flowers appear in small clusters bearing round berries which are purple when ripe. They have a sweet pungent taste and an intense scent. The fruit are picked before they are fully ripe to preserve their aroma, and then dried in the sun.

Because this species is dioecious, male and female plants must be planted together. Once the tree is five or six years old, it bears fruit for the first time; after fifteen years it reaches its peak and from then on it lives on for one hundred years. The leaves and the fruit of the tree contain the essential oil eugenol, as well as tannin and resin. Used in an infusion it alleviates indigestion.

The spice is used in pastries, with vegetables, meat, sausages, salads, herring, broths, sauces and many other dishes. In South America it is used to lend aroma to **cocoa**. **Allspice** is used in cosmetics and soaps.

PIMPINELLA ANISUM	Aniseed

Family: *Umbelliferae*
Origin: *the Middle East*
Height: *23.6 inches (60 cm)*
Flowering: *August*
Properties: *antispasmodic, sedative, digestive, expectorant, stomachic*

Aniseed is cultivated all around the Mediterranean. It is renowned since antiquity for its digestive properties. In Egypt and Rome the seeds were chewed after heavy meals to prevent indigestion; hence, the tra-

Aniseed

The leaves of aniseed are used to season salads, fruit and vegetables. They can be added to fresh sauces or served chopped to season salmon. The seeds are used in Indian cuisine to enhance the flavor of soups and fish. In Italy and Germany they are added to bread and to strong gingerbread dough. Aniseed lozenges are a very popular remedy for coughs. Furthermore, aniseed is used to give aroma to many alcoholic beverages like the French Pastis, the Turkish Raki, the Egyptian Zibiba, the Italian Sambuca, the Greek Ouzo, the South American Aguardiente, the Spanish Anisette ...

dition of serving **aniseed** desserts at the end of banquets. Today it is grown almost everywhere. The most important cultivation countries are France, around Angers and Bordeaux, Spain, India, Turkey and Germany.

This annual, aromatic plant does not propagate in the wild. It is grown from seed in April. It shrives in nourishing, permeable ground in a sunny location.

The plant has long stalked basal, teethed leaves and shorter stalked stem leaves. Its inflorescences produce magnificent small white flowers which form loose umbels.

The fruit, or seed, is greenish-grey, nearly ovoid in shape, long and with five longitudinal dorsal ridges. Before the seeds are ripe, the whole plant is pulled out of the earth and hung in order to dry. Then, the small seeds are knocked off and spread out to dry in the shade. **Aniseed** seeds have a sweet perfume and a strong taste similar to that of **licorice**.

Aniseed contains a fatty, fragrant oil as well as a blue essential oil which is used in Germany in order to dye spirits.

This plant also has medicinal properties. It alleviates stomach ache, facilitates digestion, soothes cramps, helps fight nervousness and sleeplessness, and works as an expectorant. Earlier, **aniseed** was believed to have rejuvenating and detoxifying effects.

In India **aniseed** is used for eau de toilette. Furthermore, it is used to mask the unpleasant flavors of certain medicines.

PIPER CUBEBA, PIPER LONGUM, PIPER NIGRUM	Cubeba, Black pepper, White pepper

Family: *Piperaceae*
Origin: *India, Indonesia, Sri Lanka, Malabars coast*
Height: *32.8 feet (10 m) and more*
Flowering: *spring*
Properties: *antiseptic, anti-nausea, carminative, digestive, diuretic, hemostatic, stimulant, tonic,*

Pepper thrives in tropical climates. The plant is a woody climber which holds on to trees by means of its aerial roots. Its broad, shiny green, ovoid, pointed leaves are alternately arranged.

The small flowers appear in dense, slender spikes of about 50 blossoms each. The berrylike fruit,

or **peppercorns**, are green at first and become red at maturity. **Black**, **white** and **green pepper** come from the same plant.

Green pepper is obtained by harvesting the fully grown but still unripe berries. Directly after they are harvested they are placed in brine, so that they do not turn brown.

Black pepper is none other than the whole yellow berries which are harvested shortly before full maturity and set to dry in the sun for several weeks.

White pepper is obtained by partially removing the outer part of the pericarp from the full ripe, red berries. Removal is done first by trampling in salted water, or by torrefaction in steam, and later by washing and rubbing.

These three kinds of **pepper** differ in their taste: **white pepper** is less pungent and less aromatic than **black pepper**; **green pepper** is mild and slightly sweet. Ground **pepper** is frequently grey because it contains a mixture of white and black corns. Therefore, its taste is both pungent and aromatic.

The **pepper** plant prospers in tropical regions and climates in nutritious, damp, but well drained ground in partial shade. The plant is propagated by stem cuttings, which are set out near a tree or a pole to serve as a support.

When the **pepper** plants are approximately ten feet high, they are trimmed to facilitate their harvest. At the age of five years, the plant bears fruit for the first time, and continues bearing fruit every three years for another ten to twelve years.

There are other varieties of plants which are related to **black pepper**. **Cubeba pepper** (*Piper cubeba*) is the fruit of a plant that grows in the wild. The fruit are harvested before they are ripe and are dried in the sun. This **pepper** has the same characteristics and is used in the same way as **black pepper**, but its flavor is aromatic and slightly bitter.

Piper longum was used by the Greeks and Romans. Today, however, it is hardly found. The taste resembles that of **black pepper**, but is sweeter and slightly sour.

Pepper contains 5 to 10% piperine, oils and essential oils as well as resins. For a long time it has been highly valued in traditional medicine because of its healing properties. It stimulates the appetite, alleviates nausea and toothaches, promotes digestion and stops external bleeding.

Pepper

Pepper is found along with salt on tables throughout the world. It is present in almost all dishes to enhance other flavors. Black pepper is used in stews, salads, grilled and braised meat, fish and certain cheeses, like cheddar. White pepper is used to season vegetable purées, pastries, and white sauces. Green pepper goes well with grilled fish, chicken, duck and other meat dishes. It is also used in mayonnaise and egg salads. The wild peppers are an ingredient in mixed spices like ras-el-hanout and curry preparations.

PRUNUS MAHALEB **Mahaleb cherry**
Family: *Rosaceae*
Origin: *the Middle East*
Height: *16.4 to 19.6 feet (5 to 6 m)*
Flowering: *spring*
Properties: *tranquilizer, laxative, sedative*

This tree produces a fruit which resembles a cherry, known under the Arab name of **mahaleb**. It is found in the mountain forests of the Middle East, and in France, frequently in the Vosges Mountains.

The **mahaleb** tree has a straight, cylindrical trunk with smooth bark. Its branches, arranged in a rounded shape, have stalky, sharp, oval leaves. The white flowers arranged in clusters of six to eight flowers, bear small, ovoid, bitter fruit which are at first green and then black when ripe.

The spice, **mahaleb**, is obtained from the dried nuts of the fruit. Commercially, they are found whole, as dried yellow grains, or crushed into a white powder.

Mahaleb contains not only a volatile, yellow oil which is heavier than water, mineral salts and vitamin B, but also hydrogen cyanide which in large amounts can be extremely toxic. For this reason, the spice is used moderately in the kitchen.

The **mahaleb** nut is used in perfumery to produce an essence, obtained by crushing the nut, placing it in water and distilling it, which is used in soaps and several cosmetic products.

PUNICA GRANATA   **Pomegranate**

Family: Punicaceae
Origin: West Asia
Height: 13 to 26 feet (4 to 8 m)
Flowering: summer
Properties: astringent, febrifuge, mineralizing, tonic

This tree is spread throughout most tropical and subtropical regions, in India and all around the Mediterranean. The latin name *Punica* goes back to the time when the Romans gained the tree after their victory against the Carthagians at the end the Punic Wars; *granata* refers to the numerous seeds the plant has. The Moors introduced the tree to Spain, and in turn the Conquistadors took it with them to America.

The **pomegranate** tree is a small tree with a bent trunk. It has elliptic to lance shaped, bright green, rough leaves. It has beautiful, single, red, trumpetlike flowers borne toward the ends of the branches in clusters of four to five.

The fruit is the size of a large orange covered with a thick, rough, orange-red pericarp which is crowned by the divisions of the calyx of the dead flower. Inside the fruit is divided into several chambers containing many thin, transparent vesicles of reddish, juicy, sweet and sour pulp each surrounding an angular, elongated seed.

The seeds contain water, vitamin C and various mineral salts.

The reddish-grey bark of the **pomegranate** root is used as a purgative and vermifuge. Its dried flowers have antiseptic properties.

Its seeds are used as a spice, and its juice serves as a substitute for **lemon** juice in vinaigrettes and sauces. **Pomegranate** syrup is used to add scent to beverages, sweets and pastries. The fresh seeds are also used as an ingredient for desserts and fruit salads. Dried in the sun or in the oven, **pomegranate** seeds are used

crushed into a powder to season eastern dishes giving food a slightly sour taste.

The tannin found in the rind of the fruit is used in tannery; the pigment of the bark is used to color wool. In art, an open **pomegranate** full of seeds is not only a symbol for friendship and unity between two people, but also of death.

RHUS CORIARIA   **Sumach**

Family: Therebinthaceae
Origin: the Middle East, Mediterranean region
Height: 6.5 to 9.8 (2 to 3 m)
Flowering: spring
Properties: carminative, digestive, febrifuge, stimulant, tonic

---

Sumach, which has been used since antiquity, is a compact shrub which can be found throughout Italy and the Middle East, and whose berries are used as a spice. In the past, it was used by the Romans instead of vinegar or **lemon**; in eastern dishes it is used as a substitute for **tamarind**. Its delicate leaves take on a extraordinarily beautiful red coloring in autumn.

The white flowers appear in terminal clusters and bear red fruits which are harvested shortly before maturity and dried in order to conserve them for a longer period of time. **Sumach** has a weak aroma and a pleasant sour taste.

Sumach is rich in tannin, mineral salts, and vitamins B and C. **Sumach** not only alleviates fever and digestive problems, but it is also used as a tonic to stimulate the whole body.

In Lebanon it is used as a spice in several dishes and as an ingredient in zhatar, a mixture of spices. In Syria, Turkey, and Iran it is used to enhance savory dishes. The berries are used whole, ground, or crushed.

When used whole, they are soaked in hot water and pressed to extract a juice which is used in marinades, stuffings or sauces. They can also be added to a ragout shortly before it is served. The powder is not only used as a spice for fish, poultry, grilled meat and rissoles, but also for green bean, potato, cucumber and beetroot salads. **Sumach** goes well with almost every vegetable. In Central Europe it is used with raw onions.

Finally, because **sumach** contains tannin, it is used in tanning.

Mahaleb

Mahaleb seeds are used ground as a spice for doughs and cake mixtures. They can also be used for sauces, fish, braised dishes, and game. Besides they are used to perfume jams and fruit salads. In Turkey mahaleb is used to spice mutton and vegetables, and occasionally in order to give aroma to teas. So that the spice does not lose its aroma, it is kept in an airtight container in a cool, dark place. Its exotic fragrance and taste resemble that of bitter almonds and cherries.

SACCHARUM OFFICINARUM,   *Sugar cane*
BETA SACCHARUM   *and Sugar beet*

Family: *Gramineae and Chenopodiaceae*
Origin: *India and Central Europe*
Height: *16.4 to 29.5 feet (5 to 9 m) and 23.6 inches (60 cm)*
Flowering: *summer*
Properties: *laxative, nutritious, mineralizing, stimulant, tonic*

Sugar is a sweet spice which is obtained from different plants, mainly from **sugar cane** and **sugar beets**. **Sugar** and **salt** are the most important and the oldest natural means of preserving food. Pliny and Dioscorides considered **sugar** a sort of honey, which was contained in the pith of certain types of reed, that could be kept cold and frozen like **salt**, but evidently the Romans did not know how to refine **sugar**. Refined **sugar** came to Europe with the Crusaders, and the Venetians held its monopoly for many years.

By the end of 14th century, **sugar cane** was introduced to Sicily and Cyprus. A century later, it came to Spain where it propagated very quickly. Today this valuable plant is cultivated in almost all warm countries. Provided the climate allows it, its culture is one of the most important and profitable ones: the **sugar** content of **sugar cane** is more than 15%.

Resembling a giant reed, **sugar cane** grows in clumps of solid stalks with regularly spaced nodes with a bud at each node. The graceful, sword-shaped leaves can reach up to 6.5 feet long and fall off as the plant ages. The sheath folds around the stem, protecting the bud. When the cane becomes mature, a growing point at the upper end of the stalk develops into a slender arrow, bearing a tassel of tiny white flowers that yields oblong seeds. There are, however, some sorts of **sugar cane** which are sterile and produce no fruit.

Once the flower blooms, the plant withers very quickly, becoming heavy, brittle and yellow: it must then be harvested. After the harvest the stalks are divided in two parts: one, which has no leaves, known as **sugar cane**; the other, known as cane head or cane arrow, provides green leaves and is used as cuttings to obtain a new plant.

After the stalks have been chopped and cooked, the substance is filtered, cooled and chilled; thus, crystallized **sugar** is obtained. This **sugar** is washed and the honey, fatty, brown juice is removed to produce raw **sugar**. To obtain refined white **sugar**, raw **sugar** is purified once more. **Sugar cane** contains saccharose, amino acids and mineral salts which make it a plant high in energetic value.

The second plant from which **sugar** can be extracted is the **sugar beet**. Originally from Silesia, **sugar beet** was introduced to France in 1815 by **Mathieu de Dombasle**. **Sugar beet** is a large, conical root with a light colored flesh and white rind. **Sugar**, identical to that of **sugar cane**, is obtained from its juice.

Sugar beet contains 96% of juice from which 10 to 15% of **sugar** can be extracted. **Sugar** is obtained by a process identical to the one used with **sugar cane**, and is then refined.

Sugar beet contains betaine and glutamic acid. It stimulates the activity of the liver cells and plays an important role in the functioning of the brain. It is found as a fine powder, crystallized, and in chunks. It is used to prepare sweet, hearty dishes, caramel, sweets, jams and crystallized fruits.

Sugar reduces sour and bitter aromas, it enhances certain flavors, and is used in liqueurs, ice cream and syrups. Consumed in large amounts, it is unhealthy: it causes cavities, inflammation of the gums, and diabetes. Diabetics must take saccharin, an artificial **sugar** substitute. There is, however, a plant from which a type of **sugar** is produced known as *stevia rebaudiana* which is well known in Japan and Paraguay. The dried, chopped, cooked leaves of this plant produce a powder similar to **sugar** which can be safely used by diabetics. This plant has a promising future.

SANTALUM ALBUM   **Sandalwood**

Family: *Santalaceae*
Origin: *India, Ceylon*
Height: *26.2 to 32.8 feet (8 to 10 m)*
Flowering: *after the rainy season*
Properties: *antiseptic, stimulant, sudorific*

Even if **sandalwood** is not a spice in the real sense of the word, it is a precious wood valued because of its fragrance and its medicinal properties.

It was not until the end of 19th century, that traditional European medicine began to show an interest in this species.

Sandalwood

Sandalwood is popular in the East as a perfume. Ground to a powder it is roasted or mixed with rice paste; it is also used to make incense and candles. A volatile, extremely light oil, which has a characteristic odor, is obtained through distillation. In Asia this oil is sold as an imitation of rose essence.

White **sandalwood** is a parasitic tree which hooks itself on to the roots of surrounding trees. It has leathery leaves in pairs, each opposite to the other on the branch. It carries tiny clusters of flowers which render berries the size of cherries.

When the tree is approximately ten years old, it is cut down and its yellow brown wood is put to use. The wood has an intense, pleasant scent which resembles that of a mixture of rose and musk.

This scent is used in medicine and perfumery. Its very aromatic oil, obtained by steam distillation of the wood, is used in Asia to imitate rose essence.

SASSAFRAS ALBIDUM

Sassafras, Ague tree

Family: Lauraceae
Origin: United States
Height: 98.4 feet (30 m)
Flowering: spring
Properties: anti-rheumatism, stimulant, sudorific, tonic

The **sassafras** tree is a large, aromatic tree with varying foliage: its red veined leaves, which have a shining, green top side and a bluish, green underside, can be – often on the same twig – either three lobed, mitten shaped, or entire. In autumn their color is shiny yellow, orange or purple.

The tree has a furrowed, thick and aromatic bark. Its yellow-green male and female flowers are small and without petals. They stand in small clusters and develop themselves into ovoid, intensely blue drupes.

The parts of the plant that are used are the leaves and the roots which are rich in an essential oil containing safrole.

Sassafras stimulates sweat; thereby, promoting the elimination of toxins in the organism. The dried leaves prevent the deterioration of perishable foods.

Sassafras

A decoction from the wood of the root is used to alleviate rheumatism. The infusion from the leaves of the plant stimulates and tonifies the organism.

SCHINUS MOLLE

Pepper tree, Peruvian or California pepper tree

Family: Anacardiaceae
Origin: South America
Height: 49.2 feet (15 m)
Flowering: spring
Properties: anti-inflammatory, antiseptic, purgative

The **pepper tree**, also known as **Peruvian** or **california pepper tree**, is an attractive, feathery evergreen. It has long, alternating, compound leaves with about forty lance-shaped leaflets. The entire foliage is quite aromatic because the leaves have storage cells that contain a volatile oil.

The inconspicuous, white flowers are borne in clusters at the end of the branches. Each small, pealike,

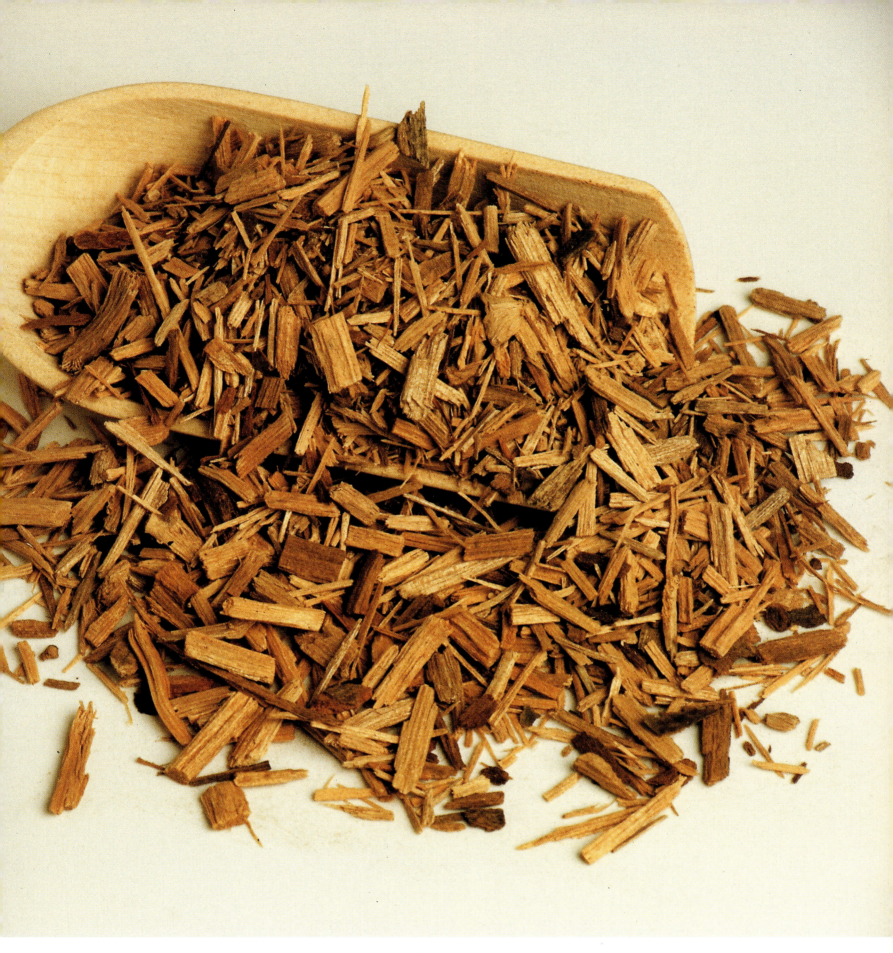

coral-red, berrylike fruit has a hard kernel surrounding one seed. This seed is covered by a pulp which, once dry, looks like parchment.

The tree is easily cultivated and grows well in dry regions like Mexico where it is planted as a shade tree. It has recently arrived in Réunion where it is valued for its production of pink **pepper** which became fashionable with Nouvelle Cuisine.

The berries are harvested shortly before they reach full maturity and are dried in the sun or immersed in brine. The taste of **Peruvian pepper** is slightly aromatic, sweet, with a peppery, bitter after taste. Occasionally the berries are also used as a substitute for **black pepper** (*Piper nigrum*).

They contain a great amount of volatile oils, resins and woody tissues. One of the resins of the pepper tree makes for a great purgative; its leaves are used in the treatment of abscesses in the mouth, and its pulverized bark alleviates edema.

In the kitchen, the seeds of **Peruvian pepper** are used to produce vinegar and beverages resembling wine. A pinch of **Peruvian pepper** can be added to season fish and seafood dishes.

A very appetizing spice is obtained by mixing the **Peruvian pepper** grains with other sorts of **pepper**. However, it should be taken into account that due to its components **Peruvian pepper** can be toxic in large amounts.

From the berries, an essence used in perfumes is obtained; from its wood, tannin; and from its leaves, a yellow color. Its aromatic and fragrant resin is also named American mastic and is used in the production of chewing gum. Its dried fruits are frequently used in dry bouquets and flower arrangements because they remain attached to the panicle for a long time.

are whitish or pink to reddish. The fruit are tiny, long flat, pear-shaped capsules containing numerous small seeds. Despite the fact that these seeds contain a large amount of oil, they are almost odorless. However, when roasted, they release a sweet fragrance and a pleasant nutty taste.

Sesame is a very useful plant because it is very rich in proteins, and the seeds contain up to 40% of a fragrant, edible oil. Due to its contents, the plant also possesses medicinal properties. A decoction made with its leaves is used for eye baths; in a compress, they alleviate inflammation.

Sesame can also be used as a purgative to cleanse and soothe the organism. Moreover, it is a very nutritious food, and its oil resists oxidative rancidity.

The press cake remaining after the oil is extracted is rich in proteins and is used as livestock feed. **Sesame** is also used in perfumery and in the pharmaceutical industry to produce soaps, cosmetic products and lubricants. The Chinese burn the oil to make soot for the finest Chinese ink blocks.

SESAMUM INDICUM   **Sesame**

Family: Pedaliaceae
Origin: tropical Africa
Height: according to species 23.6 inches (60 cm) to 6.5 feet (2 m)
Flowering: after the rainy season
Properties: emollient, laxative, strengthening, mineralizing

Sesame

Crushed sesame seeds are used to prepare a spicy paste called tahini, which is frequently used in Middle Eastern cooking; thinned with water, it constitutes taratoor, a sauce that is eaten as a dip with Arab bread; and mixed with ground chickpeas it is used for hummus, another hors d'œuvre dip. The seeds, whole or ground are used in sweet and savory dishes, breads, biscuits and sweets. In Japan, there is gomasio, a mixture of ground sesame seeds and salt. It is used in sushi, with fish, and in tempura. Sesame oil is very popular in Asian dishes and is also used to make margarine. There is also halva, a Middle Eastern confection made of crushed and sweetened sesame seeds in honey or sugar. The ground seeds can be added to pancake dough. In West Africa, the young shoots and leaves of the plant are eaten as a vegetable.

Sesame seeds are used as a cereal, a seasoning and to produce a prized edible oil. Probably originating in East Africa, it quickly spread to West Asia, India and China. It was already cultivated in Mesopotamia 2300 BC. The Chinese used it 5,000 years ago.

Today **sesame** is grown in many countries and the majority of the harvest is used on the spot – for example, in India, Burma, Pakistan, Turkey, China, Mexico, Guatemala, in the southeast of the United States, and in Uganda. The main exporting countries are Nigeria and Sudan. The annual world production is approximately 20 million metric tons of seeds.

There are different sorts of **sesame**: white, brown and black.

Sesame is an annual plant which depending on the species may or may not have branches. The velvety, leaves are undivided, teethed or largely lobed, alternate or opposing depending on the variety. One to three flowers appear on the leaf axils. They have waved edges and

---

SODIUM CHLORIDE   **Salt**

Family: Mineral
Origin: sea salt and rock salt
Properties: emollient, antiseptic, mineralizing

Salt is classified as a spice, even though unlike all other spices, it is not of vegetable origin. Because **salt** is composed of chloride and sodium, it is an essential element to the body's health; daily recommended **salt** intake is 0.28 oz. (8 gr.).

In Europe, white **salt**, from the Mediterranean, is washed and sold in grains of different sizes. On the Atlantic Ocean, **salt** is collected by hand from large coastal marshy swamps. The sea water which settles in these swamps contains approximately 3% of **salt** which is obtained by evaporation. This **salt** is grey and, because it is submitted to no other treatment, more natural than refined **salt**. Fine sea **salt** is obtained by passing the brine through a series of crystallizing pans and later dried. **Salt** is colorless, water-soluble, and is found in the form of white, sharp-edged crystals. **Salt** has been used for centuries as a seasoning and to preserve food.

Since antiquity **salt** is one of the most important trade goods and has been obtained using the same

procedures as today. According to **Pliny**, **salt** swamps could be found on the island of Crete and in some coastal regions of Italy and Africa.

During the Roman empire, underground springs were exploited for **salt**. **Salt** has also played an important role in different cults and rituals of ancient nations: Israelites used it during sacrifices to purify and, occasionally, **salt** was also added to holy water.

Due to the fact that **salt** consumption increased, most governments had the idea of imposing a tax on it or monopolizing its trade. In France, in 1340 under **Philippe IV** a tax on **salt** consumption, known as the *gabelle*, was imposed. It was only abolished in 1790. In 1806 a new tax on **salt** was issued; despite its profitability, it was abolished in 1848.

Even though **salt** has been used as a seasoning for centuries, its chemical composition was only discovered during the 18th century. Besides its use in the kitchen, **salt** – rock **salt** in particular – has a number of different applications. It is used to thaw snow and ice, to soften water, to manufacture silage and fertilizers, textiles, glass, pottery and leather. It also has medicinal applications: a **salt** solution is used as a mouth rinse in order to disinfect abscesses in the oral cavity and alleviate sore throats; as a footbath it refreshes painful, tired feet.

In the kitchen, **salt** is used in kernels or refined and is kept in an airtight container in a dry place. Pure **salt** enhances the taste of many foods.

No recipe manages without **salt**. Some dishes even require it in large amounts, for example, raw fish marinated in brine. It is used for processing pickles, preserving and curing fish, meat and some vegetable products.

Black **salt**, whose grey color acquires a tone of pink when ground, is used in India to give meals a smoky taste. In Mexico, Tequila is served in a glass rimmed with **salt** (and lime juice) to underline the taste of the beverage.

Tamarind

Tamarind is available in slices, dried, as a paste, as a fruit concentrate, or as a beverage. The juice of the fruit can be obtained by: soaking the dried slices in lukewarm water; dissolving the paste in hot water for about 10 minutes and passing it through a sieve; or, dissolving six tablespoons of the concentrate in hot water. In the Middle East and in the Antilles, tamarind juice is used to prepare a refreshing beverage. It is also used in the production of syrups, sweets, and liquid seasonings like Worcester sauce. In Réunion, a sour rice dish is prepared with the pith of the full-ripe picked fruits. It is not only used to make jams, jellies, and fruit pastes, but also to season beans and lentil dishes. In Thailand, the pith and the flowers are used as an ingredient for kaeng som, a bitter, pungent soup. The flowers, which also have a sour taste, can be consumed raw, mixed with sweet crab's paste or chili sauce. The ripe fruit can be eaten fresh, or as an ingredient in Prik Ka Krie (a mixture of chili, salt and sugar). Tamarind can be preserved in honey or sugar. The roasted ripe seeds cooked in water produce a beverage similar to coffee.

TAMARINDUS INDICA	**Tamarind**
Family: *Leguminosae*	
Origin: *East Africa*	
Height: *65.6 to 82 feet (20 to 25 m)*	
Flowering: *after the rainy season*	
Properties: *antiseptic, laxative*	

Although **tamarind** comes from Africa, the tree is cultivated very frequently in Asia and recently also in America.

Its an evergreen with alternate, pinnately compound leaves; the 12 to 25 single leaflets fold themselves at night. Its beautiful, yellow flowers with orange veining are borne in terminal clusters. The fruit is a brown plump, elongated pod that does not split open. It

contains flat, black seeds embedded in a soft, yellowish pulp. This portion of the fruit is what is known as **tamarind**.

The name goes back to the original Arab name *tamâr hindi* which means Indian date, because the Arabs compared this pith to the pulp of dried dates. It has a weak fragrance, but a distinct sweet and sour, fruity, refreshing taste.

The **tamarind** fruit contains carbohydrates (40%), organic acids (maleic acid, among others), calcium and phosphorus. The pulp is used to make a drink, is eaten fresh and is an ingredient of Worcestershire sauce. The fruit is said to improve digestion, relieve gas, sooth sore throats, and act as a mild laxative.

Due to their acidity, the ripe fruit can be used to clean copper and brass objects.

THEOBROMA CACAO **Cocoa**

Family: *Sterculiaceae*
Origin: *Mexico, South America*
Height: *26.2 feet (8 m)*
Flowering: *after the rainy season*
Properties: *stimulant, diuretic, tonic*

TRIGONELLA FOENUM-GRAECUM **Fenugreek**

Family: *Leguminosae*
Origin: *India, southern Europe*
Height: *3.9 to 23.6 inches (10 to 60 cm)*
Flowering: *April to July*
Properties: *apéritif, carminative, emollient, laxative, stimulant, tonic*

The **cocoa** plant is a small tropical tree worshipped during pre-Columbian times by the native people of Mexico who called it food of the gods. The seeds contained in the fruit were harvested with great care, since they were considered to have the same value as gold.

The Aztecs, and later the Toltecs, already cultivated the tree and knew how to dry, roast and grind the beans. This powder was mixed with maize, **vanilla** and **pepper** to produce a beverage which the Aztec ruler **Moctezuma** appreciated very much. **Cortés** discovered the beverage and presented it to the Spanish king, **Charles V**, in 1528. The aristocracy found the new aroma to be delightful; nevertheless, they replaced the **pepper** with sugar. The beverage remained a secret for almost one hundred years before its introduction to France.

It was not until the 19th century that the Swiss began to produce chocolate bars. In 1828, the Dutchman **Conrad van Houten** patented a process to extract **cocoa** butter from ground and roasted **cocoa** beans. At beginning of the 20th century, a Frenchman discovered chocolate powder. Today, chocolate can be found with all kinds of different aromas.

The **cocoa** plant is a small, evergreen tree with **cinnamon**-colored bark whose white wood is light and brittle. Its green, lance-shaped leaves are alternate and divided into fingerlike leaflets. The numerous, small flowers in whitish-green are borne in clusters directly on the branches. After pollination, the flowers bear numerous, small, oblong fruit which are colored red when ripe. They have a rough rind and inside they are divided in segments containing the seeds, which are the size of a bean and are surrounded by a fleshy membrane. **Cocoa** beans contain stimulating alkaloids like caffeine and theobromine which is a diuretic substance.

Cocoa butter is used industrially in the production of medical ointments and cosmetics. The theobromine, which is extracted from the seeds and the rind of the fruit, is used in the production of diuretics.

Fenugreek, a fine spice, whose seeds have a delicate celery fragrance, is a plant that gives off a scent similar to that of freshly mowed hay. This legume was already known to the Greeks and the Egyptians who called it *helbeh*.

Fenugreek is used as a food, a seasoning and a medicine. It is a hardy plant which thrives in temperate, dry regions. The plant is erect, loosely branched with trifoliate, light green leaves.

In the spring, small white flowers are borne alone or in clusters on the axils of high leaves. They bear slender pods, which are curved and beaked, containing 10 to 20 seeds.

After the harvest, the fruit are set to dry and shaken to loosen the seeds which have a bitter taste and a fragrance similar to that of celery. They contain essential oils, phosphorus, trigonelline, different vitamins and minerals.

Traditionally considered an aid to digestion, **fenugreek** is successfully used in the treatment of stomach problems and fever.

Because it contains vitamins and minerals, it strengthens the metabolism and helps fight against anaemia. Because of its effect on fat metabolism, it is given to treat unnatural weight loss. Used externally in a compress, the seeds soothe abscesses and reduce cellulitis.

As a spice, **fenugreek** is hardly known in western preparations, however, it is frequently used in India and Africa. Because its seeds are very hard, they are ground and added to ragouts, pastries, and spice mixtures like curries, pickles and chutneys. They can also be cooked and crushed.

The leaves of the young shoots can be added to salads or, finely chopped, in cauliflower, carrot or potato gratins. In Egypt and Ethiopia, this spice is an ingredient in bread and other national dishes. **Fenugreek** produces a coloring matter used to give textiles a very attractive red color, and oil.

Cocoa

Fresh cocoa beans are bitter and contain a vegetable fat known as cocoa butter. To become edible and before being ground, cocoa beans must be fermented, dried and roasted. Only then can they be used in the production of chocolate. Cocoa contains lipids (25%), carbohydrates (65%), mineral salts (iron, magnesium) as well as vitamin A and B$_2$. Because of its gentle, bitter taste cocoa is a popular ingredient in confectionery. Chocolate is one of the most famous and favorite aromas worldwide.

UNCARIA OR NUCLEA GAMBIR

Uncaria or Gambier

Family: Rubiaceae
Origin: India and Malaysia
Height: 32.8 feet (10 m) and more
Flowering: after the rainy season
Properties: antiseptic, stomachic, tonic

The **uncaria** is a climber from tropical regions with red-brown bark and simple, rough opposing, oval, pointed leaves. The flowers are borne in round, globular or terminal inflorescences bearing capsulelike fruit.

The leaves and the twigs are harvested and cooked, decocted and evaporated to produce a resin which resembles **catechu** and is known under designations like **pale catechu**, **terra japonica**, or **gambier**. The odorless resin has a reddish-brown coloring and an antiseptic, bitter taste. It has, however, a very bleak consistency and can be softened with the heat produced by ones hands. Fothergill used **gambier** in 1758 for the first time in medicine. The resin consists mainly of tannin and is given as an infusion or in tablets against dysentery and diarrhoea. It is also used to fight stomach weaknesses. Moreover, it reduces the secretion of the glands and stops the production of mucus. In the kitchen it is hardly used except occasionally mixed with betel **pepper** to be chewed.

VANILLA FRAGRANS

Vanilla

Family: Orchideaceae
Origin: Mexico
Height: 98.4 feet (30 m)
Flowering: spring
Properties: aphrodisiac, febrifuge, stimulant, tonic

Of the numerable orchid species, **vanilla**, which is mainly used as a fragrance, is the only one used in human nutrition. The plant is a climbing vine whose blossoms are naturally pollinated only by a bee which is found in Mexico. Up to the 19th century, it was cultivated exclusively in this country. It was only until after 1841 that its cultivation was made possible in other warm countries. **Vanilla** consumption in Europe increased once pollination was done artificially outside of the plant's natural environment.

Vanilla

Vanilla has a fine taste and a sweet, flowery scent which goes very well with sweets, cakes and other desserts. It is used to spice marmalades, ice cream, milk pudding and chocolate. It is used in the production of liqueurs made with eggs, cocoa, coffee, cocoa cream and galliano. When vanilla pods are kept in an airtight container with icing sugar for three to four weeks, a deliciously perfumed sugar is obtained, which is used to make pastries. In the modern kitchen, vanilla is occasionally used for savory dishes. In the cosmetics industry, it is used in the production of perfumes and rice powder.

The principal sources of **vanilla** are Madagascar, the Comoros, and Réunion, but it is also cultivated in Indonesia and Uganda. Nowadays, Madagascar furnishes approximately three quarters of the world's supply. The island produces bourbon **vanilla**, which is the most popular and expensive **vanilla** due to its extraordinary fragrance. **Vanilla** is the fruit of a vigorous climber which has been known to man for centuries: the Aztecs used it to flavor their chocolate beverage. But it was not until 1520, with the arrival of the Conquistadores in Mexico, that it became known worldwide. Since the 16th century, **vanilla** is the most important spice used in chocolate production.

The **vanilla** plant is a tropical orchid with a long fleshy stem that attaches itself by aerial rootlets to trees. The leaves are evergreen, elliptical, and very fleshy. The greenish-white, inconspicuous flowers stand in small clusters on the axils of the leaves. They bear thin capsules or pods of about 11 inches long which look like green beans. Inside each pod, there are ten thousand tiny seeds.

The bean pods take up to eight months to mature. As soon as they turn golden green at the base, the unripe beans are harvested. The beans are then soaked in hot water – between 140 °F and 158 °F (60 to 70 °C) – for about two minutes. Then they are set to drain in a heated chamber for twelve hours. Afterwards, they are left to dry in the sun for two to three weeks until glucose and **vanilla** are released. Then the pods are sorted and set to dry completely in the shade. After being graded, they are gathered in bundles, wrapped in wax paper, and stored till they are sold two to three months later.

The dark brown color of the fermented **vanilla** pods is obtained through oxidation; they contain 1.3 to 3% of pure vanillin which deposits in tiny, whitish crystals on the skin giving them a hoarfrost appearance. This coating is known as *givre*. Generally, the yield is rather low; a **vanilla** plant supplies approximately 17.6 oz. of **vanilla**.

To cover the large demand, a synthetic **vanilla**, which is obtained from the woody parts of the plant has been developed; however, its aroma is not to be compared to that of natural **vanilla**.

Rich in essential oil and benzoic acid, **vanilla** has a strengthening effect: it promotes the function of the digestive organs, strengthens the stomach and supports the building of tissue. It is also known to be an aphrodisiac. An infusion from the pods is often used to lower fever.

> **VITEX AGNUS CASTUS**   **Chaste or Monk's pepper tree, Wild lavender**
>
> **Family:** *Verbenaceae*
> **Origin:** *south Europe, Mediterranean region*
> **Height:** *19.6 feet (6 m)*
> **Flowering:** *late summer*
> **Properties:** *anaphrodisiac, astringent, sedative, stimulant*

The **chaste tree** is a shrub from the Mediterranean area which was already known to the Greek. In former times, it also played a role in monastic life: the seeds were mixed in with the food of the monks, who also often carried amulets made from its wood to protect themselves against temptations of the flesh. Thus, its name *Agnus castus*, **chaste lamb**, **chaste tree**, or **monk's pepper**.

The tree's branches are thin and whitish. The alternating, palmate, leaves are velvety on the top side and produce very fragrant, violet flowers in tight clusters of up to twelve inches (30 cm) long. The round fruit or drupes have a strong scent and a hot, pungent taste. This shrub thrives in hot climates and dry, light ground.

The fruit, which are harvested in autumn, can be served fresh or dried in the shade and kept in an airtight container to be used ultimately as a spice.

The fruit contain essential oils, tannin, alkaloids, flavone and cumarin. The **chaste tree** inhibits the central nervous system and controls the hormone activity. Thus, having both a sedative and stimulant effect on the organism. It is rich in essential oils.

In the kitchen, it can replace **pepper**, but its taste is less intense. It enhances sauces, stuffings, pastries and stews, and is a nice spice for meat and game. Its brittle twigs are used in Greece and Italy to make baskets. The shrub also makes for a decorative garden plant.

> **XYLOPIA AETHIOPICA**   **Guinea pepper**
>
> **Family:** *Anonaceae*
> **Origin:** *African west coast*
> **Height:** *about 49 feet (15 m)*
> **Flowering:** *all year round*
> **Properties:** *digestive, stimulant, stomachic, tonic*

The fruit of this aromatic, tropical tree have long been used as a spice and a medicine. **Guinea pepper** is also known under the name "grains of paradise." In Europe this spice has been used since the 12th century when it arrived on the back of a camel of a North African caravan and then loaded onto ships to the south of France.

The tree has entire, elongated, oval, rough, dark green leaves. It carries large flowers arranged in terminal, hanging clusters from which very aromatic fruit develop. They contain resins and essential oils. Their scent is intense and their taste weaker than that of **pepper**.

In the kitchen, the spice is used to lend aroma to meat and vegetables. In England, in the 16th century, beer was spiced with **guinea pepper**. It is important to note that in India there is a similar spice, **cardamom**, also known as "grains of paradise," which belongs to a different botanical family, but which has similar uses.

> **ZANTHOXYLUM PIPERICUM**   **Japanese pepper**
>
> **Family:** *Rutaceae*
> **Origin:** *China*
> **Height:** *19.6 feet (6 m)*
> **Flowering:** *summer*
> **Properties:** *analgesic, anti-rheumatic, digestive, stimulant, stomachic, tonic*

Japanese pepper is the fruit of a small tree of slim, upright form which is to be found in the Asian high forests and brushwoods.

The trunk has a grey bark and is covered by conical excrescencies: during the tree's lifetime, the thorns of the trunk become hard causing these rough, conical outgrowths. Its branches, covered with flattened thorns, have long, pinnate leaves. These are covered with aromatic glands and up to eleven entire, shiny green, dented leaflets.

The main veins of the leaves are generally thorny on the back side. The green flowers have a regular form and have numerous petals and stamens. Standing in short terminal clusters, they develop themselves into small, very aromatic, globular fruit with a hard rind. At first green, they become red when ripe. Once dry, they disintegrate, releasing black, glossy seeds.

Despite the fact that the whole plant is aromatic, only the leaves and the fruit are used. Once the fruit have been harvested, they are dried. The black, bitter

---

Japanese pepper

This spice stimulates the appetite, while a decoction with its bark and its fruit facilitates digestion and alleviates rheumatic pain. The powder can be applied to a cavity to alleviate toothache. Japanese pepper has a taste which resembles that of a mixture of pepper and aniseed. It is used in the Chinese and Japanese kitchens very frequently. It goes well with meat, fish and vegetables, and is used as an ingredient for the five spice powder. The roasted seeds have a more intense taste, similar to that of pepper. In Japan, the tree is called Hoa-Tsio which means "flower of pepper" due to its fragrance and its taste. There, the leaves are also harvested, dried and ground to prepare a traditional spice known as sansho.

seeds are removed and ground into a powder – **japanese pepper**.

This spice has a pungent aroma similar to that of **aniseed** with a touch of **lemon**. It contains essential oils, tannin, resins and flavonoid and is also used in several medical preparations.

ZINGIBER OFFICINALE   *Ginger*
Family: Zingiberaceae
Origin: India, China
Height: 3.2 to 5 feet (1 to 1.5 m)
Flowering: summer
Properties: anti-rheumatic, expectorant, aphrodisiac, tranquilizer, carminative, digestive, stomachic, stimulant, tonic

---

This spice has been cultivated for a long time in the Far East. Arab traders brought it to Greece from where it spread throughout Europe. The greek physician Dioscorides mentions some of the medical properties of **ginger** in his work *De Materia Medica*.

In the Middle Ages, **ginger** was the second most important spice after **pepper**. In the 13th century, Arab traders in eastern Africa discovered this aromatic rhizome. Later, the Portuguese would import it to West Africa. The Spanish took it with them to Jamaica and the Antilles, where the best **ginger** ever was produced.

Today, **ginger** is cultivated largely in India, China, Taiwan, Nigeria, Jamaica, the island of Mauritius and Australia. The spice is valued all over the world, however, the English are the main European consumers.

Ginger is a herbaceous, perennial plant with a fleshy rhizome and spectacular flowers. It only blossoms in the tropics. The leaves are long, elongate, alternate in two vertical rows, and arise from sheaths enwrapping the stem. The flowers are borne in terminal clusters in dense, conelike spikes and composed of overlapping green bracts which may be edged with yellow. Each bract encloses a single, small, yellow-green and purple flower. Fruit develop only rarely in the form of small capsules with three segments in which tiny black seeds lie.

Ginger is propagated by planting rootstock cuttings in rich, humid soil in the spring. Eight to ten months later, around February, the aromatic rhizomes are harvested before new shoots are formed.

Ginger may be unscraped, partly scraped, or peeled. Most of the time it is dried and shredded into pieces or ground into powder.

Ginger can be preserved by boiling in syrup or pickling in vinegar. It can also be crystallized in a syrup and rolled in sugar.

Ginger has a slightly biting taste with a refreshing touch of **lemon**. It contains a volatile oil, gingerol,

---

Ginger

Fresh ginger is used mostly with curry. It is used to season many Eastern dishes and goes well with pork, duck, beef, seafood, poultry, roasts, pastries, salads, soups and sweet and sour sauces. The Japanese marinate it in sugared vinegar and use it as a seasoning with sushi and with aperitifs. Powdered ginger is used in curry mixtures, cakes, gingerbread, and pastries. Wine, beer, like ginger beer, or ginger ale and other beverages are spiced with ginger.

Following pages
Incense

These spicy, aromatic substances come from Arabia. Since the time of Queen Saba they are considered to be particularly precious and regardless of faith, they have a sacred use. They are not edible substances.

and starch. **Ginger** is also used for medicinal purposes. It can be massaged directly on the affected area or used in a compress to alleviate arthritis, rheumatic pain and headaches. It is also good against stomach aches and toothaches. It has altogether positive effects on the digestive system and is used to strengthen vision. Traditional Chinese medicine has recommended ginger for well over 2,500 years.

As a spice in teas, it promotes blood circulation and relieves colds, coughs and influenza. Crystallized **ginger** is a popular remedy against sea sickness and travel sickness. In former times, it was also used as an aphrodisiac.

In fact, professors at the Ecole de Salerne stated: *"Every person should consume ginger regularly in order to love and be loved like in his or her youth."*

Spice Mixtures and Pastes

Powdered Spices

Cajun

This spice mixture is very popular in Louisiana. The name is derived from a distortion of the word "acadien" which was used to refer to the French Canadian people who settled in Louisiana.

Mix the following ingredients: a teaspoon of black peppercorns, cumin seeds, roasted and ground white mustard seeds, allspice, dried oregano, salt, a finely chopped onion, two spoons of paprika, dried thyme and two garlic cloves.

Cajun is the classic spice for the famous Jambalaya with Gombo. It can also be used to rub meat, fish and poultry before roasting or grilling.

Chutney

This typically English mixture combines sweet and spicy aromas. It consists, mainly, of dried fruit, green tomatoes or mangoes.

Cut the green tomatoes or mangos into pieces. Then add the same amounts of cleaned and diced apples, finely chopped onions, crystal sugar and two crushed cloves of garlic.

Place the mixture in a pan and cook. Place a tablespoonful of salt, and three tablespoons of pickling spices in a muslin bag, and hang in the mixture.

Add about 20 fl. oz of apple vinegar. Bring to the boil and allow to simmer for about one hour.

Pour the hot chutney into sterilized glasses and cover. After a month of storage, it can be eaten with meat, poultry, vegetables, or cheese.

Five Spice Powder

This aromatic spice mixture from China is added frequently to soy sauce to prepare traditional poultry dishes, grilled pork spareribs or marinades.

Take equal amounts of the following spices, grind them to a powder and mix: Sichuan pepper, cinnamon or cassia, fennel seed, star aniseed and cloves.

The dominating aroma and taste should be that of star aniseed.

Bengali Five Spice Powder

This is a variation of the previous recipe.

Fennel seeds, cumin, fenugreek, black cumin and white mustard seeds are mixed in equal parts, without roasting or grinding to a powder.

To season a dish, a portion of the mixture is fried in oil or butter, until it releases its aroma.

Colombo

This mixture, which resembles curry, is well known in the Antilles. It enhances the flavor of poultry and fish.

The powder consists of chili pepper, turmeric, mustard seeds, coriander seeds, and garlic, all carefully ground together.

Curry

For a long time the word curry, outside of India, meant any dish with an Indian sauce. In reality, curry is a mixture of several spices whose combination varies from region to region. The differences between the curry sorts arise from the ingredients which are available in the respective regions. The main thing is that the mixture must be well balanced and compatible with the base recipe.

In a pan without fat or oil, roast the following: allspice, black mustard seeds, black peppercorns, cumin, coriander and fennel seeds.

Stir constantly. When the fragrance of the spices is released and the seeds are evenly roasted, remove them from the pan. Add turmeric and ginger and carefully grind the mixture in a mortar.

Curry of the Seven Seas

or

Indonesian Curry

*This gentler mixture is suitable
for braised dishes, sambals, kebab,
various curry dishes as well as Malayan
and Indonesian dishes.*

In a pan heat white peeled cardamom seeds, coriander seeds, celery, cumin, cloves and crushed cassia bark. Grind the roasted spices to a fine powder and mix with ground allspice.

Singapore Curry

*This recipe goes particularly well
with meat and poultry.*

In a big pan without fat, brown the cumin, fennel, pepper, coriander seeds and cloves. Once all the spices are roasted, add small pieces of cinnamon and peeled cardamom capsules.

Crush all the spices to obtain a powder and add turmeric powder.

In order to use this preparation with fish, leave out the cardamom, cloves and cinnamon and add fenugreek instead.

Garam Massala

*Massala means "mixture," and "garam" means
hot or burning. Indeed, Garam Massala
is a very spicy and pungent mixture.
Depending on the region
where it is prepared, it may contain
from six to twelve spices.*

This classic mixture is made by roasting the following spices: four tablespoons cumin seeds, one tablespoonful black peppercorns, six tablespoons coriander grains, ten cloves, a cinnamon stick, ten cardamom capsules and three bay leaves.

Stir the mixture until it becomes fragrant. Remove the cardamom capsules and crumble the cinnamon stick.

Add a tablespoon of pulverized mace and grind everything to a fine powder.

Garam Massala is a good spice for sauces prepared for meat and poultry.

It may be sprinkled over a dish shortly before serving, or incorporated in a recipe.

Kam

*This is a Moroccan mixture
consisting of five spices.*

In a pan, brown two teaspoons of powdered ginger, turmeric and black peppercorns.

Add half a teaspoonful of grated nutmeg and a cinnamon stick.

Crush all ingredients to a fine powder.

This mixture goes well with mutton, chicken, fish and vegetable dishes.

Kashmir Massala

*This mixture is a very popular
seasoning for fish,
crabs and lamb.*

The ingredients are: one tablespoonful of black peppercorns, one tablespoonful of cloves, one tablespoonful of cumin, twelve green cardamom capsules, two teaspoons of caraway seeds, one teaspoonful of grated nutmeg and a cinnamon stick.

Peel the cardamom capsules and crumble the cinnamon stick.

In a pan, roast all spices except the nutmeg. When the mixture becomes fragrant, remove the cardamom capsules.

Grind everything finely and add the grated nutmeg.

Massala for Fruit Salad

*This spicy powder is used
for exotic fruit salads consisting
of papayas, mangoes, guavas,
apples and bananas.*

The ingredients and amounts for the basic recipe are: one teaspoonful of black peppercorns, ajowan, dried pomegranate seeds and cumin. Grind everything to a fine powder.

Under constant stirring, add one teaspoonful of salt and mango powder, a quarter teaspoonful of asafetida, as well as half a teaspoonful of garam massala and cayenne pepper.

This mixture for fruit salads doesn't keep.

Peanut Mixture

*This mixture is used to bread chicken,
lamb, meatballs and fish.
It should not be mistaken for
peanut butter which is a paste,
but not a mixture of spices.
The recipe is quite simple.*

Take about 2 oz. peanuts, half a teaspoonful of ground allspice, one teaspoonful of four spice powder, and salt.

Chop the peanuts coarsely.

Then mix with the other ingredients.

The mixture can be stored for about two months in an airtight container.

Ethiopian Mixture

*This complex mixture consists
of a dozen spices
whose taste and origin
are quite different.*

In a pan, place eight crushed cardamom capsules, a dozen red chili peppers peeled and without seeds, one teaspoonful of coriander seeds, cumin, allspice, fenugreek, ajowan, two teaspoons black pepper and eight cloves.

Heat stirring constantly.

Once the seeds are roasted, remove from heat. Remove the cardamom husks.

Grind the spices to a fine powder adding half a teaspoonful of grated nutmeg, one teaspoonful of ground ginger and two teaspoons salt.

This mixture is suited to fish and poultry.

Gingerbread Mixture

*This English mixture is also suitable
for cakes, puddings and pies.*

Take one teaspoonful of cloves, allspice seeds, a piece of a cinnamon stick, some coriander seeds and crush to a powder.

Mix well and add one teaspoonful of ground cinnamon, ground ginger and grated nutmeg

Mixture for Pickles

This is an English spice mixture.

The ingredients needed are: one tablespoonful of cloves, coriander seeds, allspice seeds, white peppercorns, white mustard seeds, a piece of cinnamon stick, a piece of ginger root and two or three dried red chili peppers.

This mixture can be prepared in three different ways. Cover the spices with vinegar and slowly bring to the boil.

Allow them to cool and filter.

In this way a spiced vinegar is obtained which can be used to season various foods.

It is also possible to place the spices in a muslin bag to be used when necessary depending on the recipe.

Finally, the spices can be placed in an airtight container, covered with vinegar, and left for two to three days.

Filter and use as a seasoning or condiment.

Sambaar Powder

This powder, consisting of spices and dried legumes, is known as dal in India.
It has a spicy, nutty taste
and it is used to season lentils, fresh vegetables,
sauces for meat dishes and aromatic broths.

In a pan, brown two tablespoons cumin seeds, six tablespoons coriander seeds, two teaspoons black peppercorns, fenugreek seeds, and eight to ten dried red chili peppers without seeds.

Remove the spices from the pan and set aside. Prepare the dried legumes in the same way using two tablespoons mung dal (yellow lentils), two teaspoons channa dal (split yellow peas), and urad dal (chickpeas).

Mix the spices and the legumes together and crush them into a fine powder, gradually adding two tablespoons ground turmeric.

Four Spice Powder

This typically French mixture is used
to flavor meat and stews.

The ingredients needed are: five teaspoons ground black pepper (can be replaced with three tablespoons ground white pepper), two teaspoons nutmeg, one teaspoonful of ground cloves and grated ginger (which can be replaced with cinnamon). Mix all the ingredients carefully.

Ras-El-Hanout

This mixture was created by spice traders.
Each of them had a personal recipe
consisting of up to twenty different spices.

In spite of the numerous individual modifications there is a basic recipe. Take the following ingredients and grind them into a fine powder: red chili peppers, cayenne pepper, guinea pepper, allspice, black pepper, ginger, galanga, mace, cloves, cardamom, cinnamon, turmeric, coriander, dried rose petals, dried lavender flowers, dried Iris root, and dried deseeded hot peppers.

This intensely fragrant mixture is used to season onion puree, rice dishes, tajine, couscous, ragouts and vegetable dishes.

Sancho

This is a delicate Japanese mixture.

The main ingredient used is dried ground japanese pepper leaves. Despite its name, the plant is not a pepper plant. The spice powder is used to season various traditional Japanese dishes. It can only be found as a ready-made powder in the stores.

Shichimitogarashi

This is also a traditional Japanese mixture,
consisting of six spices.
As a rule, it is used together
with soy sauce.

In a pan, roast black peppercorns, sesame seeds, black mustard seeds and poppy seeds. When the seeds are golden brown and begin to give off their aroma, add dried mandarin peel and sancho powder, and crush into a fine powder.

This very popular mixture serves as a spice for numerous Japanese dishes.

Zahtar

This mixture is used in the kitchens
of Lebanon, Syria and Iraq.

In a pan, roast sesame seeds, coriander seeds, cumin seeds, hazelnuts and a piece of roughly chopped cinnamon.

When the spices begin to give off their aroma, place in a mortar and crush, adding thyme and sumach powder obtained from the ground cornelian cherry.

Spice Pastes and Sauces

Zahtar can be used as an hors-d'œuvre, spread on bread with olive oil, or with cream cheese. It can also be used to season lentil dishes and mutton ragouts.

Baghar

This is a mixture of various spices and essences cooked in mustard seed oil. Warm baghar is served with salads in a yogurt sauce, green vegetables, or legumes. The recipe for this mixture varies according to the region.

Fry the following ingredients in mustard seed oil: black mustard seeds, assafetida and dried orange jasmine leaves. According to taste, add dried red pepper and garlic.

Coriander Baghar

This mixture is a variation on the previous one.

Heat some mustard seed oil in a pan and fry some chopped onion and cumin seeds. While the vegetables are still white, add fresh coriander leaves. Serve with soup or with vegetable dishes.

Allspice Candy

A spicy delicacy.

Mix bean puree with bananas: heighten the taste of the paste by adding ginger powder, onion puree and a fresh chopped red hot pepper. Mix again. Roll in to small balls and set to dry.

Harissa

This paste is used in North Africa with meat and vegetable tajines, kebab, hors-d'œuvres, and to flavor couscous. Mixed with fresh tomato puree it becomes a seasoning for grilled meat. It can also be added to ragouts and soups. With curd milk, it is used to marinade chicken, lamb and fish.

Soak a dozen dried chili peppers in hot water. Once they are soft, dry them. Mix them with two cloves of garlic, one teaspoonful of dried mint and one teaspoonful of salt and pound them to a paste.

In a pan without fat, roast two teaspoons coriander seeds, a teaspoonful of caraway and a teaspoonful of cumin. When the spices are golden yellow and begin give off their aroma, crush them to a fine powder.

Mix the pepper puree with the crushed spices, gradually adding olive oil, until it becomes a smooth paste. Harissa should be stored in a jar in the refrigerator with some olive oil over the top to seal it.

Madras Massala

This is an Indian spiced sauce made with fresh and dried spices.

In a pan, roast eight tablespoons coriander seeds, four tablespoons cumin, one tablespoonful peppercorns and one tablespoonful of black mustard seeds.

When the spices begin to be fragrant, remove them from the heat and crush them to a fine powder.

Add eleven tablespoons turmeric powder, one tablespoonful of salt and three teaspoons pulverized, dried red pepper powder.

Mix and add eight crushed garlic cloves, freshly grated ginger, and apple vinegar. A thick paste should be obtained.

To intensify the aroma, the sauce may be cooked in an oiled pan stirring until most of the oil has been absorbed.

Green Massala

This green sauce is relatively mild and refreshing. It is used with crab, fish, chicken and other poultry. It also flavors rice and noodles.

In a pan, roast ten split, green cardamom capsules and six cloves until they give off their aroma. Grind to a fine powder, and add two teaspoons turmeric powder and just as much salt.

Mix the fenugreek seeds; which have soaked in water overnight, with four cloves of garlic, a piece of freshly grated ginger root, about 2 oz. (50 gr.) of fresh coriander leaves, fresh mint and some apple vinegar.

Mix the paste thus obtained with the powdered spices. Pour the mixture into a hot pan containing 3.38 fl. oz. of a mixture of sesame and sunflower oil.

Stir until the oil begins to sizzle.

Allow the massala to cool, and pour it in a jar covering it with a thin layer of oil to preserve its color and aroma.

Curry Paste Mus-sa-man

This Asian spice paste is well suited to meat, poultry, fish and vegetables.

Cut and heat fresh red hot peppers together with shallots, four cloves of garlic, galanga and lemon grass, to intensify their aroma. Mix everything to obtain a fine paste and add fresh coriander leaves, the zest of a cedrat or grapefruit as well as shrimp paste.

Aside, in a pan, quickly heat up some coriander seeds, cumin, crushed cardamom capsules, and salt. Remove the cardamom capsules, add cloves and cinnamon and mix into a fine powder.

Mix the prepared paste with the spice powder thoroughly to obtain a homogeneous paste.

Thai Curry Paste

This spice paste is quite pungent and is also well suited to meat, poultry, fish and vegetables.

This preparation adds a pretty red color to food. In a pan without fat, roast cumin and coriander seeds. When brown grind into a powder. Prepare a puree with some oil, fresh red hot peppers, red onions, garlic, lemon grass, galanga and some fresh coriander leaves.

Pour this puree into the mixer and add the grated peel of a citron or grapefruit, shrimp paste, and salt. Slowly add the cumin and coriander seeds. The curry paste can now be used. It is also possible to keep it for three to four weeks in an airtight container in the refrigerator.

Green Curry Paste

The preparation is similar to that of the Thai curry paste above.

Proceed as explained above, but instead of red peppers, use green peppers and white onions instead of red; the fresh coriander leaves give the paste its appetizing color.

Malayan Spice Paste

It is a delicious paste suitable to chicken curries.

Mix twelve shallots, four garlic cloves, a piece of chopped, fresh turmeric root, a cube of shrimp paste and ten macadamia nuts into a smooth paste.

Slice three lower stems of lemon grass into rings, add them to the mixture and stir. This mixture can be kept in the refrigerator in an airtight container for a few days.

Sambal with Shrimp Paste

It is a sauce which is used in small amounts to spice rice and vegetable dishes.

To make this sauce, take fresh red hot peppers cut lengthwise and salt, put them in a mortar with salt and pound them. Add the juice of a lemon and a little shrimp paste to give the sauce an intense aroma.

Spice Pastes and Sauces

Sambal Kecap

*This Indonesian sauce can be used
as a substitute for the peanut sauce
which is generally used with fried chicken
and other meat dishes.*

Mix a chopped red hot pepper with two cloves of garlic, two tablespoons tamarind juice and two tablespoons hot water. According to taste, fried onions can also be added.

The sauce should be left to stand for a half an hour before serving.

Red hot Pepper Sambal

*Known in Indonesia as sambal ulek,
this sauce can be kept for long periods
of time; therefore, it can be prepared
in large amounts.*

Blanch red hot peppers in boiling water for five minutes. Puree the peppers and add a little salt.

This spice paste should be used in small amounts because it is very hot.

It goes well with meat and poultry dishes.

Nam Prik Sauce

*This is a very popular Thai sauce
that can be served with rice dishes,
used as seasoning or as a sauce
with raw vegetables.*

Mix about 2 oz. of shrimps, three cloves of garlic, some shrimp paste, some fresh coriander leaves and three chopped red hot peppers without the seeds.

Add four tablespoons lemon juice, approximately three tablespoons fish sauce and a tablespoon brown sugar.

To obtain a lighter sauce, add a little water.

Soy Sauce

*This sauce, which is very popular
in Asian cuisine, is known all over the world.
According to the kind of soy beans used,
its taste, color and intensity varies.
Soy sauce is used alone or mixed
with other spices or seasonings
such as hoisin sauce, oyster sauce
or shoyu sauce.*

This sauce is made by cooking the previously ground soy beans, mixing them with wheat flour and fermenting them with koji (fermented rice). After a while, a black aromatic, fragrant juice – soy sauce – is obtained.

Tabasco

*The name Tabasco is actually
an American brand name
which was originally given to a pepper sauce.*

This sauce is made with red hot peppers which are pureed with vinegar and salt. Tabasco is used to season soups, fish, meat and poultry. However, this hot sauce also goes well with eggs, omelettes and gives tomato juice more bite.

Tadka

*This rather simple sauce is used
in oriental cuisine.*

In a covered pan, melt two tablespoons butter. Add two tablespoons black mustard seeds and cover to prevent the seeds from jumping out of the pan. Remove from heat and add half a teaspoonful asafetida powder and eight fresh or dried orange jasmine leaves.

Pour this sauce into soups, over meat, into ragouts or vegetable dishes.

Crocus.

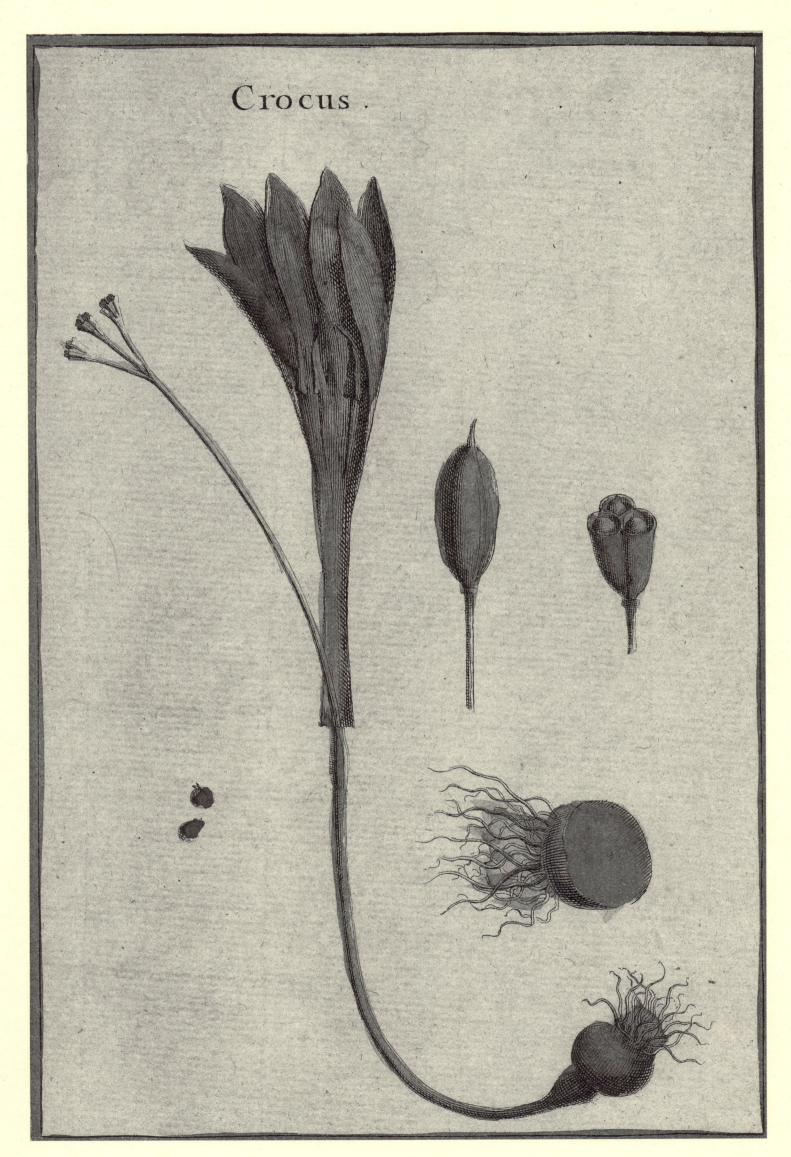

INDEX OF LATIN NAMES

ACACIA CATECHU: **cutch, betel palm** 22
AGATHOPHYLLUM: **ravensara, Madagascar, clove nutmeg** . . 22
ALEURITES MOLUCCANA: **candle nut tree, tung tree** 24
ALPINIA GALANGA: **greater galanga** 24
ALPINIA OFFICINARUM: **lesser galanga** 26
ANETHUM GRAVEOLENS: **dill** 26
ARENGA PINNATA: **arenga, sugar palm** 26
ARMORACIA RUSTICANA: **horseradish** 28
ASARUM EUROPAEUM: **wild ginger, asarabacca** 30

BETA SACCHARUM: **sugar beet** 102
BIXA ORELLANA: **annatto** 30
BRASSICA ALBA, B. JUNCEA, B. NIGRA: **mustard** 32
BROSIMUM GALACTODENDRON: **cow tree, milk tree** 74

CAPPARIS SPINOSA: **caper bush** 34
CAPSICUM ANNUUM: **bell pepper** 36
CAPSICUM TETRAGONUM: **paprika** 38
CARICA PAPAYA: **papaya** 39
CARUM AJOWAN: **ajowan** 40
CARUM CARVI: **caraway** 40
CARYOTA URENS: **toddy palm** 42
CASSIA FISTULA: **cassia** 42
CHASMANTHERA PALMATA, C. COLUMBA: **calumba** 44
CINCHONA LANCIFOLIA, C. OFFICINALE, C. SUCCIRUBRA:
China bark, cinchona 44
CINNAMOMUM CAMPHORA: **camphor** 46
CINNAMOMUM CASSIA: **Chinese cinnamon** 48
CINNAMOMUM ZEYLANICUM: **Ceylon cinnamon** 48
CITRUS AMBLICARPA, C. HYSTRIX: **wild lemon, combava** 50
CITRUS AURANTIIFOLIA: **lime** 50
CITRUS AURANTIUM: **Seville orange, sour orange** 50
CITRUS BERGAMIA: **bergamot** 52
CITRUS LIMON: **lemon** 52
CITRUS MEDICA: **citron** 54
CITRUS SINENSIS: **sweet orange, common orange** 54
CLEOME HASSERLIANA: **cleome, spiderflower** 56
COFFEA ARABICA: **coffee** 56
COLA ACCUMINATA: **cola** 58
CORIANDRUM SATIVUM: **coriander** 58
CORNUS MAS: **cornelian cherry** 60
CROCUS SATIVUS: **saffron** 60
CUMINUM CYMINUM: **cumin** 63
CURCUMA DOMESTICA: **turmeric** 62
CURCUMA ZEDOARI: **shell ginger** 65

DRIMYS LANCEOLATA, D. WINTERY: **winter's bark** 66

ELETTARIA CARDAMOMUM: **cardamom** 67
EUCALYPTUS GLOBULUS: **eucalyptus** 68
EUGENIA CARYOPHYLLATA: **clove** 70
EUGENIA UNIFLORA: **Surinam cherry** 72

FERULA ASA FOETIDA: **asafetida** 72
FOENICULUM VULGARE: **fennel** 72

GALACTODENDRON: **cow tree, milk tree** 74
GLEDITSIA TRIACANTHOS: **honey locust** 75
GLYCINE MAX: **soy bean** 76
GLYCYRRHIZA GLABRA: **licorice** 78

ILLICIUM VERUM: **star aniseed** 80

JUNIPERUS COMMUNIS: **juniper** 80

MANGIFERA INDICA: **mango** 82
MONODORA MYRISTICA: **Jamaica or Calabash nutmeg** 84
MONSTERA DELICIOSA: **philodendron, ceriman** 84
MORINGA OLEIFERA: **horseradish tree** 86
MURRAYA KOENIGII: **orange jasmine** 86
MYRICA GALE, M. RUBRA: **sweet gale, bog myrtle** 86
MYRISTICA FRAGRANS: **nutmeg and mace** 88
MYRTUS COMMUNIS: **myrtle** 90

NIGELLA SATIVA: **black cumin, fennel flower** 90
NUCLEA GAMBIR: **uncaria, gambier** 112

PANDANUS TECTORIUS: **screw pine** 92
PAPAVER SOMNIFERUM: **opium poppy** 93
PEUMUS BOLDUS : **boldo** 94
PHYLLANTHUS ACIDUS : **otaheite gooseberry** 94
PIMENTA DIOÏCA: **allspice** 96
PIMPINELLA ANISUM: **aniseed** 96
PIPER CUBEBA, P. LONGUM, P. NIGRUM:
cubeba, black pepper, white pepper 96
PRUNUS MAHALEB: **mahaleb cherry** 98
PUNICA GRANATA: **pomegranate** 100

RAVENSARA: **ravensara, Madagascar or clove nutmeg** 22
RHUS CORIARIA: **sumach** 100

SACCHARUM OFFICINARUM: **sugar cane** 102
SANTALUM ALBUM: **sandalwood** 102
SASSAFRAS ALBIDUM: **sassafras, ague tree** 104
SCHINUS MOLLE:
pepper tree, Peruvian or California pepper tree 104
SESAMUM INDICUM: **sesame** 106
SODIUM CHLORIDE: **salt** 106

TAMARINDUS INDICA: **tamarind** 108
THEOBROMA CACAO: **cocoa** 110
TRIGONELLA FOENUM-GRAECUM: **fenugreek** 110

UNCARIA: **uncaria, gambier** 112

VANILLA FRAGRANS: **vanilla** 112
VITEX AGNUS CASTUS: **monk's pepper tree, wild lavender** . . 114

XYLOPIA AETHIOPICA: **Guinea pepper** 114

ZANTHOXYLUM PIPERICUM: **Japanese pepper** 114

ZINGIBER OFFICINALE: **ginger** 116

AGUE TREE: **sassafras albidum** 104
AJOWAN: **carum ajowan** 40
ALLSPICE: **pimenta dioica** 96
ANISEED: **pimpinella anisum** 96
ANNATTO: **bixa orellana** 30
ARENGA: **arenga pinnata** 26
ASAFETIDA: **ferula asa foetida** 72
ASARABACCA: **asarum europaeum** 30

BELL PEPPER: **capsicum annuum** 36
BERGAMOT: **citrus bergamia** 52
BETEL PALM: **acacia catechu** 22
BLACK CUMIN: **nigella sativa** 90
BLACK PEPPER: **pipper nigrum** 96
BOG MYRTLE: **myrica gale, m. rubra** 86
BOLDO : **peumus boldus** 94

CALABASH NUTMEG: **monodora myristica** 84
CALIFORNIA PEPPER: **shinus molle** 104
CALUMBA: **chasmanthera palmata, c. columba** 44
CAMPHOR: **cinnamomum camphora** 46
CANDLE NUT TREE: **aleurites moluccana** 24
CAPER BUSH: **capparis spinosa** 34
CARAWAY: **carum carvi** 40
CARDAMOM: **elettaria cardamomum** 67
CASSIA: **cassia fistula** 42
CERIMAN: **monstera deliciosa** 84
CEYLON CINNAMON: **cinnamomum zeylanicum** 48
CHASTE PEPPER TREE: **vitex agnus castus** 114
CHINA BARK TREE: **cinchona lancifolia, c. officinale, c. succirubra** 44
CHINESE CINNAMON: **cinnamomum cassia** 48
CINCHONA: **cinchona lancifolia, c. officinale, c. succirubra** . . 44
CITRON: **citrus medica** 54

AND OF ENGLISH NAMES

CLEOME: **cleome hasserliana** 56
CLOVE NUTMEG: **agathopyllum, ravensara** 22
CLOVE: **eugenia carophyllata** 70
COFFEE: **coffea arabica** 56
COCOA: **theobroma cacao** 110
COLA: **cola accuminata** 58
COMBAVA: **citrus amblicarpa, c. hystrix** 50
CORIANDER: **coriandrum sativum** 58
CORNELIAN CHERRY: **cornus mas** 60
COW TREE: **brosimum galactodendron** 74
CUBEBA: **pipper cubeba,** 96
CUMIN: **cuminum cyminum** 63
CUTCH: **acacia catechu** 22

DILL: **anethum graveolens** 26

EUCALYPTUS: **eucalyptus globulus** 68
FENNEL: **foeniculum vulgare** 72
FENNEL FLOWER: **nigella sativa** 90

FENUGREEK: **trigonella foenum-graecum** 110

GAMBIER: **uncaria, nuclea gambier** 112
GINGER: **zingiber officinale** 116
GREATER GALANGA: **alpinia galanga** 114

HONEY LOCUST: **gleditsia triacanthos** 75
HORSERADISH: **armoracia rusticana** 28
HORSERADISH TREE: **moringa oleifera** 86

JAMAICA NUTMEG: **monodora myristica** 84
JAPANESE PEPPER: **zanthoxylum pipericum** 114
JUNIPER: **juniperus communis** 80

LEMON: **citrus limon** 52
LESSER GALANGA: **alpinia officinarum** 26
LICORICE: **glycyrrhiza glabra** 78
LIME: **citrus aurantifolia** 50

MACE: **myristica fragrans** 88
MADAGASCAR NUTMEG: **agathopyllum** 22
MAHALEB CHERRY: **prunus mahaleb** 98
MANGO: **mangifera indica** 82
MILK TREE: **brosimum galactodendron** 74
MONK'S PEPPER TREE: **vitex agnus castus** 114
MUSTARD: **brassica alba, b. juncea, b. nigra** 32
MYRTLE: **myrtus communis** 90

NUTMEG: **myristica fragrans** 88
OPIUM POPPY: **papaver somniferum** 93
ORANGE JASMINE: **murraya koenigii** 86
OTAHEITE GOOSEBERRY: **phyllanthus acidus** 94

PAPAYA: **carica papaya** 39
PAPRIKA: **capsicum tetragonum** 38
PEPPER TREE: **schinus molle** 104
PERUVIAN PEPPER: **schinus molle** 104
PHILODENDRON: **monstera deliciosa** 84
POMEGRANATE: **punica granata** 100

RAVENSARA: **agathopyllum** 22

SAFFRON: **crocus sativus** 60
SALT: **sodium chloride** 106
SANDALWOOD: **santalum album** 102
SASSAFRAS: **sassafras albidum** 104
SCREW PINE: **pandanus tectorius** 92
SESAME: **sesamum indicum** 106
SEVILLE ORANGE: **citrus aurantium** 50
SHELL GINGER: **curcuma zeodari** 65
SOUR ORANGE: **citrus aurantium** 50
SOY BEAN: **glycine max** 76
STAR ANISEED: **illicium verum** 80
SUGAR BEET: **beta saccharum** 102
SUGAR CANE: **saccharum officinarum** 102
SUGAR PALM: **arenga pinnata** 26
SUMACH: **rhus coraria** 100
SURINAM CHERRY: **eugenia uniflora** 72
SWEET GALE: **myrica gale, m. rubra** 86
SWEET ORANGE: **citrus sinensis** 54

TAMARIND: **tamarindus indica** 108
TODDY PALM: **caryota urens** 42
TUNG TREE: **aleurites moluccana** 24
TURMERIC: **curcuma domestica** 62

UNCARIA: **uncaria, nuclea gambir** 112

VANILLA: **vanilla fragrans** 112

WHITE PEPPER: **pipper longum** 96
WILD GINGER: **asarum europaeum** 30
WILD LAVENDER: **vitex agnus castus** 114
WILD LEMON: **citrus amblicarpa, c. hystrix** 50
WINTER'S BARK: **drimys lanceolata, d. wintery** 66

POWDERS SPICE

CAJUN .121
CHUTNEY 121
FIVE SPICE POWDER 121
BENGALI FIVE SPICE POWDER 121
COLOMBO 121
CURRY 121
INDONESIAN CURRY 122
SINGAPORE CURRY 122

GARAM MASSALA 122
KAM 122
KASHIMIR MASSALA 122
MASSALA FOR FRUIT SALAD 122
PEANUT MIXTURE 123
ETHIOPIAN MIXTURE 123
GINGERBREAD MIXTURE 123
MIXTURE FOR PICKLES 123

SAMBAAR POWDER 124
FOUR SPICE POWDER 124
RAS-EL-HANOUT 124
SANCHO 124
SHICHIMITOGARASHI 124
ZAHTAR 124

SPICE PASTES AND SAUCES

BAGHAR 125
CORIANDER BAGHAR 125
ALLSPICE CANDY 125
HARISSA 125
MADRAS MASSALA 125
GREEN MASSALA 125

CURRY PASTE MUS-SA-MAN 126
THAI CURRY PASTE 126
GREEN CURRY PASTE 126
MALAYAN SPICE PASTE 126
SAMBAL WITH SHRIMP PASTE . . . 126
SAMBAL KECAP 127

RED HOT PEPPER SAMBAL 127
NAM PRIK SAUCE 127
SOY SAUCE 127
TABASCO 127
TADKA 127

BIBLIOGRAPHY

The Book of Herbs, Dawn Titmus, 2000
Les épices, Henri Leclerc, Masson, 1929
Flavoring with Spices,
Clare Gordon Smith / James Merrell, 2000
The Herb Guide, Sally Ann Berk, 2001
Herb and Spice Handbook,
Arabella Boxer, 1999
Herbs and Spices, Karen Farrington, 1999
The Herbal Pantry, Emelie Tolley / Chris Mead, 1992
The Mistress of Spices,
Chitra Banerjee Divakaruni, 1998
The Natural pharmacy,
Miriam Polunin et Christopher Robbins,
Origine des plantes cultivées,
A. de Candolle, Jeanne Laffitte, 1883
Parsley, Peppers, Potatoes & Peas: A Cook's Companion for Handling,
The Spice Routes: Chronicles and Recipes from Around the World,
Caldicott, Chris and Carolyn, 2001,
Tropical Herbs & Spices, Wendy Hutton / Alberto Cassio, 1997
Using & Storing a Garden's Bounty, Pat Katz, 2002